A Bicultural Heritage:

*Themes for the Exploration of Mexican
and Mexican-American Culture in
Books for Children and Adolescents*

by
ISABEL SCHON

The Scarecrow Press, Inc.
Metuchen, N.J. & London
1978

Library of Congress Catalog Card No. 78-4322
ISBN 0-8108-1128-6

ACKNOWLEDGMENTS

Many people have influenced the ideas that I have expressed in this book. I particularly wish to acknolwedge my sincere appreciation to Dr. José Carrera Tamborrel for his invaluable insights and guidance; to Dr. Howard Sullivan for his constant support and advice; to Mrs. Maryann Shipley for her patient corrections and recommendations; to Mrs. Elizabeth Outcalt for her gracious cooperation and assistance; to Ms. Stephanie Reith and Ms. Diane Stone for their delightful endurance and collaboration. A special note of gratitude is due to my family, professors, colleagues, and friends in Mexico City for instilling in me a reverence for Mexico and its people. I also wish to express my thankfulness to Miss Barbara Quarles, Mrs. Alida Stevens, and to the University Grants Committee, Arizona State University, which made this work possible.

CONTENTS

OVERVIEW

A Bicultural Heritage is designed to expose students
to the customs, lifestyles, heroes, folklore, and history of
Mexican and Mexican-American cultures. The readings and
activities are intended to be entertaining as well as informa-
tive. The goals are:
- To promote feelings of respect and appreciation toward
  Mexican and Mexican-American values and customs.
- To develop an awareness of the similarities and differ-
  ences between Mexican and American lifestyles.
- To increase the feelings of esteem for outstanding
  Mexicans and Mexican Americans.
- To appreciate the beauty and variety of Mexican folk-
  lore.
- To understand the heritage of the Mexican people.

The Attitude Survey following this Overview may be
used by teachers to measure students' feelings about Mexican and Mexican-American people, customs, history, folklore,
heroes, and lifestyles before and after they are exposed to
the readings and activities suggested in this book. It is
hoped that most of the goals outlined above will be attained
by as many students as possible and that there will be a
positive improvement in the attitudes of the students toward
the Mexican and Mexican-American cultures.

A Bicultural Heritage is arranged by five theme areas:
customs, lifestyles, heroes, folklore, and key historical de-

1

velopments. These five theme areas are divided into three
grade levels: kindergarten through second grade, third
through sixth grade, and seventh grade through high school.

Each of these grade level sections, in turn, consists
of the following four principal parts: 1) Outcomes; 2) Books;
3) Discussion; and 4) Evaluation and Follow-up Activities.

Outcomes: The outcomes are specific learnings that
students may be expected to acquire as a result of the readings, discussions, and activities suggested in this book.
Teachers may use the outcomes to guide students' reading
into definite areas of concern. Not all the outcomes will be
learned or acquired by all students, since not all students
will read all the books that are discussed.

Books: An attempt has been made to include as many
as possible of the books about Mexican and Mexican-American children and adolescents that are now available in school
and public libraries. But only books that are marked with
an asterisk are recommended titles. I have chosen to recommend only those books that particularly concur with the goals
of A Bicultural Heritage, listed above. Unfortunately there
are very few. Teachers should read the discussions of each
book mentioned, in order to understand my decision for recommending or not recommending a specific book. Although
many teachers and students will certainly disagree with me,
I urge readers to be especially critical of the books that I
do not recommend. There are too many stereotypes and misconceptions in the minds of many students about Mexican and
Mexican-American people to allow these books to perpetuate
untruths or half-truths indefinitely.

As any teacher or librarian knows, it is very difficult to assign a grade level to a book. And, even though I
have done so for the convenience of some teachers or students,

please use the grade level only as a tentative guideline. An
arbitrary grade level should never stop a student from reading or viewing a book that he or she expresses interest in.

Discussions: The discussions are intended to give the
readers a brief introduction to the themes into which this
book is divided and to summarize, criticize and/or highlight
specific ideas explored in books about Mexican or Mexican-
American children and adolescents. In the discussions I have
expressed my personal opinions of the books, emphasizing
what I believe are the strengths or weaknesses of each.
Also, I have pointed out misspelled Spanish words throughout
the discussions.

Evaluations and Follow-up Activities: This section
suggests informal evaluation ideas and follow-up activities.
They directly coincide with the Outcomes for each theme.
Teachers will notice that each outcome has its corresponding
evaluation or follow-up activity, with the appropriate answers
or suggestions. Because the main purpose of A Bicultural
Heritage is to interest students in the culture of the Mexicans and Mexican-Americans, the evaluations should be used
as casually as possible, so that students will not have their
reading controlled or limited by the desire to do well in the
evaluations.

PRE- AND POST-ATTITUDE SURVEY

Name (optional) _____ Sex (circle one) M   F

Age _____   Grade _____

Your race _____   Your nationality _____

Directions: If desired, write your name and fill in the other information requested above.

Each of the statements on this opinionnaire expresses a feeling which a particular person has toward Mexican or Mexican-American people. You are to express, on a five-point scale, the extent of agreement between the feeling expressed in each statement and your own personal feeling. The five points are: Strongly Disagree (SD), Disagree (D), Undecided (U), Agree (A), Strongly Agree (SA). You are to encircle the letter(s) which best indicates how closely you agree or disagree with the feeling expressed in each statement AS IT CONCERNS YOU.

SD	D	U	A	SA
(Strongly Disagree)	(Disagree)	(Undecided)	(Agree)	(Strongly Agree)

1. I'd enjoy having Mexican-American friends.

   SD   D   U   A   SA

2. Being with Mexican-Americans makes me feel uncomfortable and restless.

   SD   D   U   A   SA

3. It is all right for Mexican-Americans to intermarry with any other group.

   SD   D   U   A   SA

5

4.   Mexican-Americans do not favorably impress me.

     SD   D   U   A   SA

5.   Mexican-Americans have many undesirable characteris-
     tics.

     SD   D   U   A   SA

6.   I admire the Mexican-American culture.

     SD   D   U   A   SA

7.   Mexican-Americans are courteous people.

     SD   D   U   A   SA

8.   Mexican-Americans are disorderly in their conduct.

     SD   D   U   A   SA

9.   I do not see how anyone can be fond of Mexican-Amer-
     icans.

     SD   D   U   A   SA

10. Mexican-Americans do not deserve any respect.

     SD   D   U   A   SA

11. Mexican adults take a siesta every day.

     SD   D   U   A   SA

12. Mexican pre-Columbian objects do not interest me.

     SD   D   U   A   SA

13. The folklore of Mexico is dull.

     SD   D   U   A   SA

14. There are no Mexicans or Mexican-Americans worthy
     of my admiration.

     SD   D   U   A   SA

15.   I would be happy to have Mexican-American neighbors.

      SD   D   U   A   SA

Part 1

CUSTOMS

Grades: Kindergarten-Second

OUTCOMES

1. Name foods shown in pictures of Mexican food.

2. Describe "fun-type" activities connected with going to a market (mercado).

3. Compare Christmas celebrations in Mexico and the U.S.

4. Describe other holidays not found in children's books at this level.

5. Realize that there are stereotypes in the books about Mexicans and Mexican-Americans.

    a. That not all Mexicans or Mexican-Americans live in extreme poverty.

    b. That not all Mexicans live in quaint villages.

    c. That not all Mexicans eat only tortillas.

    d. That donkeys are not the only means of transportation in Mexico.

    e. That becoming a bull fighter is not the dream of every Mexican boy.

BOOKS*

Balet, Jan. The Fence. Delacorte Press, 1969.

*Only books marked with an asterisk are recommended titles.

Baylor, Byrd. Coyote Cry. Lothrop, Lee and Shepard
    Co., 1972.

Bolognese, Don. A New Day. Delacorte Press, 1970.

Buffler, Esther. Rodrigo and Rosalita. Steck-Vaughn Com-
    pany, 1949.

Bulla, Clyde Robert. The Poppy Seeds. Thomas Y.
    Crowell, 1965.

Clymer, Eleanor. Santiago's Silver Mine. Atheneum, 1973.

Coatsworth, Elizabeth. The Noble Doll. Viking, 1961.

Dralle, Elizabeth. Angel in the Tower. Farrar, Straus,
    and Cudahy, 1962.

*Ets, Marie Hall and Aurora Labastida. Nine Days to
    Christmas. Viking, 1959.

Fraser, James. Las Posadas. Northland Press, 1963.

Garrett, Helen. Angelo, the Naughty One. Viking, 1944.

Grifalconi, Ann. The Toy Trumpet. Bobbs-Merrill, 1968.

Hader, Berta and Elmer. The Story of Pancho and the
    Bull with the Crooked Tail. Macmillan, 1942.

Hitte, Kathryn and William D. Hayes. Mexicali Soup.
    Parents Magazine, 1970.

Hood, Flora. One Luminaria for Antonio. Putnam and
    Sons, 1966.

Kent, Jack. The Christmas Piñata. Parents' Magazine
    Press, 1975.

Kirn, Ann. Two Pesos for Catalina. Rand McNally, 1961.

*Leaf, Munro. The Story of Ferdinand. Viking Press, 1969.

Lewis, Thomas P. Hill of Fire. Harper and Row, 1971.

Martin, Patricia Miles. Friend of Miguel. Rand McNally,
    1967.

Morrow, Elizabeth. The Painted Pig. Alfred Knopf, 1930.

Nava, Julian, editor. My Friends. Aardvark, 1974.

Politi, Leo. Juanita. Scribners, 1948.

Politi, Leo. Lito and the Clown. Scribners, 1964.

*Politi, Leo. The Nicest Gift. Scribners, 1973.

*Politi, Leo. Pedro, The Angel of Olvera Street. Scribners, 1946.

Politi, Leo. Rosa. Scribners, 1963.

Prieto, Mariana. When the Monkeys Wore Sombreros. Harvey House, 1969.

Ritchie, Barbara. Ramon Makes a Trade. Parnassus Press, 1959.

Shura, Mary Francis. Pornada. Atheneum, 1968.

Sonneborn, Ruth A. Seven in a Bed. Viking Press, 1968.

Stone, Helen V. Pablo the Potter. Lantern Press, 1969.

Ungerer, Tomi. Orlando the Brave Vulture. Harper and Row, 1966.

Warren, Betsy. Papacito and His Family. Steck-Vaughn, 1969.

DISCUSSION

Food

Mexican food is very well known and enjoyed by many children. There is a great variety of Mexican dishes that some children may already be familiar with, such as "tacos," "tostadas," "arroz con pollo" (chicken with rice), "enchiladas," "pozole" (spicy soup with hominy), "mole" (meat or poultry with a very spicy sauce), "tamales," many vegetables, fruits, and desserts. Unfortunately, as discussed later under "Stereotypes: Tortillas," most books show Mexican or Mexican-American people eating only "tortillas" and beans.

The Nicest Gift, by Politi, is an outstanding book to show children the life of the people that came from "Old Mexico," with colorful illustrations of "el barrio." It tells about "tamales" and how they are cooked and that "Churros are made of sweet dough and cooked in a large kettle of boiling oil ... they look like pretzels." It mentions attractive aspects of Mexican-American life: "... the mercado is colorful and gay with restaurants and shops that sell all kinds of foods and Mexican merchandise." It has attractive illustrations of "piñatas," "payasos," and "boleros," depicted in middle-class settings.

My Friends, edited by Julian Nava, is a collection of seven insipid, dull stories for children. They are written in uninteresting, unimaginative short sentences. "One Sunday Morning" includes a forced incident about "Menudo" (pp. 42 and 46), "pan dulce" (p. 44), and "tortillas" (p. 44) for breakfast.

Mexicali Soup, by Hitte and Hayes, shows Mama happily going shopping to prepare her Special Mexicali Soup. Every member of the family objects to one ingredient being put in the soup because: "You know, Mama, they have different ways of doing things here, different from the ways of our town on the side of the mountain. I think we should try new ways" (unnumbered). Mama loses her enthusiasm and serves her family hot water: "The new Mexicali Soup! ... so simple! So quick! So easy to make...." The idea that Mexican food contains so much variety could be very well discussed through Mama's Special Soup.

Markets

Mexican markets are gay and colorful and offer many
"fun-type" activities for children and adults.   Children may
enjoy looking at the endless displays of toys and "piñatas,"
participating in different games, such as "Lotería" (a Mexican Bingo), watching clown shows, and eating good Mexican
candy, such as "cocada" or "ate," and fruits, such as
"mangos" or "papayas."   The following books include attractive illustrations of Mexican markets.   (Many other books
also have colorful market scenes.)

The Toy Trumpet, by Grifalconi, shows sandaled
Tomas, who lives in a little Mexican village, impatiently
waiting to buy a pink trumpet that he had seen at the market.
Beautiful water color illustrations depict a crowded marketplace where

> There were baskets
> And balloons
> And ribbons and beads ...
> There were pots
> And pans
> And green vegetables and
> Yellow cheeses
> And orange candies
> And ...

When the Monkeys Wore Sombreros, by Prieto, has
bright, colorful illustrations of two Mexican boys, two donkeys, four monkeys, and their adventures with their sombreros which they were supposed to sell at the market.

The Fence, by Balet, is an amusing story that describes one of the true realities of Mexico--life of the very
rich and life of the very poor.   The rich family is shown
with its servants and luxuries, the poor family eats bread
and smells the food from the rich family's kitchen.   The

beautiful and colorful illustrations add a very real Mexican flavor to the market scenes, the homes, and the judge's office.

Also notice the discussion of The Nicest Gift, by Politi, just mentioned under Food.

Holidays

Although Mexico has many different holidays, most books describe only Christmas celebrations in Mexico. Some holidays that children might enjoy hearing about are 16 de Septiembre (Mexico's Independence Day), All Souls' Day (November 1 and 2, when the dead loved ones are remembered with candies and special bread and food at the cemetery), Easter blessing of the animals, and children's birthday parties with "piñatas" and birthday cakes.

Juanita's birthday party and the Easter blessing of the animals are shown in a typical Mexican setting in Olvera Street in Politi's Juanita. There are several misspelled words in Spanish and the descriptions on almost every page show sandaled peasants, sombreros, and donkeys.

Christmas

There are several books that describe Mexican Christmas celebrations. Ets' Nine Days to Christmas is a true story about a little girl in Mexico City and her preparations for a Posada. She is anxiously expecting a "piñata" and waits impatiently for the day that finally her mother takes her to a market to choose the "piñata." The authors have described very well a typical day of a middle-class family in a Mexican city: life with a servant and their obligations, a typical Posada, and scenes of a traditional market.

Las Posadas, by Fraser, and The Christmas Piñata, by Kent, illustrate barefoot or sandaled Mexican children, tortillas, breaking the "piñata," and singing posadas in the traditional Mexican Christmas stories written for tourists. In Las Posadas, Mexican children "go to bed" on sarapes on the floor.

One Luminaria for Antonio, by Hood, is a Christmas story in a small New Mexican village. It shows all the people in town making preparations for the holiday, but Antonio has to deliver his papa's wood carvings, run errands for his mama, and help his sister. Finally Antonio has time to make just one lantern with a cracked candle and he does receive a blessing for the new year--an "ardilla roja" (a red squirrel).

Pedro, the Angel of Olvera Street, by Politi, describes the puestos, the Mexican food, the music, and the many festive activities in Olvera Street as preparations for the traditional Mexican Christmas celebrations. The story tells us that the pilgrims request posada in "your puestos." (Puesto means shop in Spanish.) This is perhaps a mistake in the interpretation of a posada. Posadas are not commercial affairs. They are strictly family and social celebrations.

A New Day, by Bolognese, shows the Christmas story in contemporary Mexican-American settings: "José and María worked on farms. They went from place to place looking for work" (unnumbered). The baby is born; people bring food; there is music and dancing; and the local police chief "... ordered the arrest of José and María for disturbing the peace." But, "... they knew they would all meet again" (unnumbered).

Stereotypes: Poverty ✓

To promote feelings of respect and appreciation toward genuine Mexican and Mexican-American values and customs, the children must be made aware of the many stereotypes prevalent in books.

Mexican and Mexican-Americans are often portrayed
as poor. The following are a few samples of the many
books that describe poverty:

Coyote Cry, by Baylor, is a beautifully illustrated
story of a young, poor, shepherd boy, Antonio, his grandfather, their dog and their feelings about coyotes. It includes a few Spanish words, "compañero," "cuidado," and
the typical menu: "... now that the beans and green chiles
and tortillas and wild honey have been eaten ..." (unnumbered).

Angelo, the Naughty One, by Garrett, shows Angelo,
a poor Mexican boy who hated baths. He ran away from
home the day of his sister's wedding so as not to have to
take a bath. He finally found a fort, and, as the soldiers
couldn't tell who he was because he was so dirty, they decided to give him a bath. The illustrations show typical
small town Mexican scenes, not Mexican city scenes as the
story mistakenly states.

Seven in a Bed, by Sonneborn, is a repetitive, uninteresting story of a big family of seven children who just
arrive in the big city. Papa came "... ahead of the family
to get a job...." They had to be crowded in one room and
all the children had to share one bed: "Back home they
slept two and sometimes three in a bed." In the following
eighteen pages, the children are shown trying to go to sleep
on the bed but not being able to until the father gets angry
and numbers their position in bed.

Stereotypes: Life in a Mexican Village

There are innumerable books that show sandaled peasants with sombreros and sarapes who live in small Mexican villages. The stories usually describe barefoot children accompanied by a donkey, peasants going to a fiesta, and/or children too poor to afford a much-desired toy or thing. Children should realize that there are many big, beautiful cities in Mexico, too. I will discuss just a few books of the many that show life in a Mexican village: Rosa, by Politi, is a Mexican girl who wishes she had a beautiful doll, but, "She knew the doll was too expensive for her father to buy." The beautiful illustrations show a man sleeping on an "hamaca" in the middle of the day and attractive "piñatas" and "valeros" (Mexican toy) in typical village settings.

Politi states that "Lito lived in a small city in Mexico," but the illustrations in Lito and the Clown show a small Mexican village. The story, which is full of action and gaiety, describes the village people enjoying the carnival, Payaco, the clown, and Lito's kitten. The Spanish word "Grazias" [sic] is misspelled.

Hill of Fire, by Lewis, is a simple story about the birth of the Paricutín Volcano. It shows Pablo's father working in his field every day and complaining that "Nothing ever happens." And then a hill of fire began to grow in their cornfield. The illustrations show the simple and poor life of the villagers and their meals: "Every morning for breakfast he ate two flat cakes of ground corn" (p. 10).

The Poppy Seeds, by Bulla, shows a Mexican valley where all the village people, except old Antonio, had to carry water from the river to their houses. Pablo decided to plant poppy seeds by every house to make the valley beautiful.

All the seeds dried up in the ground, except Old Antonio's, who was now very happy to see red poppies in his backyard. Antonio, in gratitude, asked the people to help him dig a ditch for all of them to have drinking water and to water a small garden in each yard.

Pablo the Potter, by Stone, has attractive Mexican village scenes and, Pablo, who had seen a red toy car with rubber tires: "If only he had enough money to buy it...." Pablo tried to earn money by lugging heavy suitcases "... for the turistas," and by selling little molded animals.   Pablo was ready to buy his long-cherished toy, when he saw his brother crying because he had dropped the candy he was going to sell, and "Knowing that he could do something useful seemed more important than the little red car."   So Pablo bought the candy from his brother.

The Painted Pig, by Morrow, is a story about Pita and Pedro in a Mexican town and their wishes to obtain another painted pig for Pedro.   The text narrates the children's conversations with the town's toymaker, and their feelings about making their own toy pig.   The vivid illustrations show the typical village scenes, "a little Indian girl who lived in Mexico ..." and "... never had a centavo to drop into the hole ..." (p. 3).   Also, as is to be expected, "... eating tortillas under his big umbrella ..." (p. 12).

Friend of Miguel, by Martin, has colorful illustrations of sandaled and barefooted peasants with sombreros and sarapes.   Miguel's grandmother prefers to "... wash our clothes at the river where I can talk to my friends" (p. 12). Miguel has a great desire to own Santiago, the horse, but "Rent for this horse and the food that we eat take all the pesos and centavos that you and grandfather earn" (p. 27). Finally, Miguel was delighted when the horse was left with him for safekeeping.

Stereotypes: Tortillas √

In many of the books about Mexicans and Mexican-
Americans, the people are shown eating only "tortillas," be-
cause they are too poor to eat anything else (see section on
Food, p. 10).

Santiago's Silver Mine, by Clymer, describes the extreme poverty of two families who do not have enough to eat
("Not even tortillas"), their fathers are constantly looking
for work, Santiago's mother has to sell her rebozo, and his
sister has to play in the dirt. "... [W]e ate our supper of
tortillas and beans" (p. 10), but when they lived in Mexico
City "... it was a shack, much worse than our house, and
twelve people lived there" (p. 13). Only foreigners are
shown driving cars, and "Andreas said, 'If only we had a
burro!'" (p. 44).

Rodrigo and Rosalita, by Buffler, is a story about a
Mexican family and the children's dreams about their father's
great artistic ability. It emphasizes the family's poor beginnings in Mexico: "Yes, Rodrigo, and I could put on my
worst raggy dress and a very, very sad face and beg for
some money from the rich Americans!" (p. 16); their meals:
"That evening for supper the family had the same old beans
and tortillas ..." (p. 22). And a woman's description of
Rosalita: "Such a quaint child. Aren't the native peasants
colorful?" (p. 45). "She's just a little beggar anyway!"
(p. 46).

Angel in the Tower, by Dralle, is a story about
Angel and his parents, the bell-ringers in a Mexican village.
It includes several silly incidents involving Angelino and the
people of his village: feeding chickens on the colored tiles
of the cathedral roof, learning to read and write a few words,

and inventing a pulley to send messages and parcels back
and forth between the tower and the square below.   Angel
only ate tortillas because "cake and fruits and milk and bread
and butter were too expensive" (p. 76).   The author wrote
this book "after a trip to Mexico," but, she writes: "No
ladies that Angel ever saw wore hats except foreign ladies"
(p. 64).   And, she exaggerates: "Many boys and girls
worked for a month as house servants for four or five pesos"
(p. 69).   The name of a Mexican President, "Venestiana
Cerranze" [sic] (p. 42), is misspelled.

Papacito and his Family, by Warren, pretends to lead
"the young reader through the daily life and language of a
Mexican family as they greet the morning, cook the meals,
do the shopping, tend the garden, wash their clothes, and
prepare for bedtime."   There are the ever-present donkey,
tortillas, frijoles, and siestas: "Maria and Beto like to eat
tortillas and frijoles for breakfast, lunch, and supper almost
every day" (p. 22).   "When it is time to go to bed, Mamacita places cuatro straw mats on the floor" (p. 30).   The
Spanish word "guitarro" [sic] (p. 29) is misspelled.

Stereotypes: Bulls and Bullfighters ✓

Several stories emphasize bulls and bullfighters in
portraying the life of Mexican people.   Children should realize that even though bullfighting is a popular pastime in Mexico and Spain, not every Mexican boy wants to become a
bullfighter, nor do bulls roam around Mexican cities.

The Story of Pancho and the Bull with the Crooked
Tail, by Hader, shows Pancho, a Mexican boy, who unex-
pectedly captured the wild bull and won the prize offered by
Don Fernando.   Pancho became the hero although many cow-

boys and riders had tried to capture the bull. Full-colored
illustrations show the typical Mexican village scenes with
adobe huts, barefooted peasants, men with sombreros and
big mustaches playing guitars, and women wearing rebozos.

Pornada, by Shura, is an amusing story of an artistic pig, Pornada, and Francisco, an artist and a dreamer.
Together they share the beauty of the mountains, the flowers,
and the river. Francisco's family is very poor, and his
father, a very practical man, insists that they sell the pig
for food. The story emphasizes the Mexican family's poverty and exaggerates: "So many miles I have traveled, so
many banditoes I have seen fade like shadows behind the
rocks of the hills, so many matadors I have passed on their
way to battle" (pp. 59-60).

The Story of Ferdinand, by Leaf, shows Ferdinand,
a delightful Spanish bull who "liked to sit just quietly and
smell the flowers." This entertaining story will please any
child and, at the same time describe to those children that
are interested, important facets of a bullfight: "Banderil-
leros," "Picadores," the Matador, scenes of the bull ring,
and sweet Ferdinand, who would not fight: "When he got to
the middle of the ring he saw the flowers in all the lovely
ladies' hair and he just sat down quietly and smelled" (unnumbered).

Stereotypes: Siestas √

Many of the books about Mexicans stress "siestas"
and insist that all Mexican adults take a siesta every day.
Children should realize that many Mexicans are hard-working people and that only in some small Mexican cities and
villages where it gets very hot in the middle of the day and

where there is no air conditioning, is a siesta a needed
rest. Siestas are not common in big cities where people
are too busy working, or in towns where the weather does
not demand a rest. The following are just samples of how
siestas are emphasized in many books:

Ramon Makes a Trade, by Ritchie, shows Ramon and
his determination to own a green parrot in a cage. Attractive illustrations show Ramon working as a merry-go-round
pusher, exchanging his jar for a sarape for his father, and
trading his father's green jar for the parrot he wanted.
And, about siestas: "He pushed during the siesta hour when
everyone, except the children, was resting in the shade"
(p. 30), with the appropriate illustration of men wearing
sombreros and mustaches.

Two Pesos for Catalina, by Kirn, is an easy-to-read
story about Catalina and her trip to market in Taxco, a city
in Mexico, with her mother and father. She searches for
just the right thing on which to spend the two pesos which
"a Tourist Lady" had given her. When they arrive, "It was
siesta time and all the fathers were napping. Their big
sombreros were pulled down over their eyes" (unnumbered).
The accompanying illustration shows all men napping on
benches on the town plaza. (Taxco is a medium-sized city
in Mexico and this scene will certainly mislead children as
to the reality of life in a Mexican city.) The typical village scenes are included, showing barefooted Indians, marketplace, donkeys, and poverty. What Catalina most wants
are "Shoes!" "Catalina had never worn a pair of shoes.
Her friends in the village had never worn shoes. Her mother seldom wore shoes" (unnumbered).

Stereotypes: Donkeys

Donkeys are constantly portrayed in books about Mexico: peasants are shown riding exclusively on donkeys, and donkeys are used as background decorations of countless village and town scenes. Although donkeys are truly part of the rural life of Mexico, children should realize that donkeys are not the only means of transportation in Mexico, nor are they an indispensable aspect of Mexican life. The following books illustrate how donkeys are used in numerous books about Mexico:

Orlando the Brave Vulture, by Ungerer, is a simple story of an altruistic vulture that searches for a lost gold miner who has gone astray in the deserts of Chihuahua. Orlando encounters a pack of Mexican bandits (with huge sombreros and sinister mustaches), "... a poor farmer who could not read" (p. 8), and barefooted peasants riding donkeys.

The Noble Doll, by Coatsworth, describes Doña Amalia, an old, lonely woman who had lost all her money, and Luisa, who came to work as Doña Amalia's servant. Luisa is shown thinking and "... eating her tortillas and beans under the shade of the Indian laurel ..." (p. 20). Doña Amalia had a beautiful old doll that used to belong to her great grandmother, which she was almost forced to sell to be able to support Luisa and herself. Vivid illustrations depict scenes in a Mexican town in which donkeys, peasants, sombreros, guitars and piñatas supposedly add "authenticity" to the story.

EVALUATION AND FOLLOW-UP ACTIVITIES

1. Ask the children to name at least four traditional Mexican foods.

2. Ask the children to describe "fun-type" activities connected with going to a market (mercado). Students
   should include at least two of the following:

   a. the colorful folk arts

   b. various shops

   c. music

   d. fruits and vegetables.

3. Ask the children to compare Christmas celebrations in
   Mexico and the U.S. The comparison of Christmas celebrations in Mexico and the U.S. should include:

   a. breaking of a piñata

   b. nine days of parties in Mexico vs. one day in the
      U.S.

   c. singing of the posadas compared to Christmas carols

   d. Nativity manger scene vs. Christmas tree.

4. Ask the students to describe different Mexican holidays.
   Children might describe:

   a. 16 de Septiembre (Mexico's Independence Day)

   b. All Souls' Day (November 1 and 2--Day of the Dead)

   c. Easter Blessing of the Animals

   d. Mexican Birthday Parties.

5. Ask the children what Mexican children would like to become when they grow up, and to describe the daily life
   of a Mexican or Mexican-American grown-up. Hopefully,
   the children will not include stereotypes in describing
   the life of Mexican or Mexican-American people. (See
   Stereotypes under Outcomes.)

OUTCOMES

1. Describe the problems of self-identity as experienced by Mexican or Mexican-American children.

2. Describe the stereotypes prevalent in the books about Mexicans and Mexican-Americans:

    a. Not all Mexicans or Mexican-Americans live in extreme poverty.

    b. Not all Mexicans eat only "tortillas" and beans.

    c. Not all Mexicans take a siesta every day.

    d. Donkeys are not the only means of transportation in Mexico nor the great treasure of all Mexicans.

    e. Not every Mexican boy wants to become a bullfighter.

BOOKS*

Arnold, Orem. The Chili Pepper Children. Broadman Press, 1960.

Beebe, B. F. Little Dickens, Jaguar Cub. Broadman Press, 1960.

Beebe, B. F. Yucatan Monkey. David McKay, 1967.

Behn, Harry. The Two Uncles of Pablo. Harcourt, Brace and World, 1959.

*Only books marked with an asterisk are recommended titles. (See also discussions of Getting to Know Mexico, by Gomez (p. 98), Mexico, by Ross, (p. 98), and Here Is Mexico, by Treviño (p. 99).

Bialk, Elisa. Tizz at the Fiesta. Children's Press, 1970.

Blue, Rose. We Are Chicano. Franklin Watts, 1973.

Brenner, Anita. The Timid Ghost. Scott, 1966.

Bulla, Clyde Robert. Benito. Crowell, 1961.

Cavanna, Betty. Carlos of Mexico. Franklin Watts, 1964.

Chandler, Edna Walker. Indian Paintbrush. Albert Whitman, 1975.

Coatsworth, Elizabeth. Daisy. Macmillan, 1973.

Coatsworth, Elizabeth. The Place. Holt, Rinehart, 1965.

Colman, Hila. That's the Way It Is, Amigo. Crowell, 1975.

Forsee, Aylesa. Too Much Dog. Lippincott, 1957.

Forsman, Bettie. From Lupita's Hill. Atheneum, 1973.

Galbraith, Clare K. Victor. Little, Brown and Company, 1971.

Gee, Maurine H. Chicano Amigo. William Morrow, 1972.

Means, Florence Crannell. But I Am Sara. Houghton Mifflin, 1961.

Nava, Julian, editor. Customs Across the Border. Aardvark, 1974.

Nava, Julian, editor. Happy Days. Aardvark, 1974.

Nava, Julian, editor. Names and Places. Aardvark, 1974.

Patiño, Ernesto. A Boy Named Paco. Naylor, 1974.

Phillips, Eula Mark. Chucho, the Boy with the Good Name. Follett, 1957.

Sawyer, Ruth. The Year of the Christmas Dragon. Viking Press, 1960.

Stolz, Mary. Juan. Harper and Row, 1970.

Tarshis, Elizabeth Kent. The Village that Learned to Read.
    Houghton Mifflin, 1941.

Titus, Eve. Basil in Mexico. McGraw-Hill, 1976.

Toepperwein, Fritz A. Jose and the Mexican Jumping
    Bean. Highland Press, 1965.

Vavra, Robert. Felipe the Bullfighter. Harcourt Brace,
    1967.

Vavra, Robert. Pizorro. Harcourt Brace, n/d.

*Villacana, Eugenio. Viva Morelia. Lippincott, 1971.

Whitney, Marion Isabelle. Juan of Paricutin. Steck-
    Vaugh, 1953.

DISCUSSION

Self-Identity

To understand the feelings of other people is no easy
task. Several authors have tried to write about Mexican or
Mexican-American children as Mexican or Mexican-American
children might experience prejudice, poverty, and/or rejection. Unfortunately, with the exception of Viva Morelia, by
Villacana, the following books do not describe the reality of
the problem of self-identity for Mexican-American children,
but rather simplify it as a language problem or solve it by
creating feeble heroes.

Viva Morelia, by Villacana, genuinely describes the
author's feelings as he is learning "about being a Mexican"
(p. 39). He was born in the state of Michoacán. He had a
Spanish father and an Indian mother. The illustrations depict middle-class homes, well-dressed children, a bullfight,

trips to several cities: Quiroga, Pátzcuaro, Janitzio, Urua-
pan, and Paricutín, school days and holidays.

Customs Across the Border, edited by Julian Nava,
is a collection of four dull stories with uninteresting characters. "A Very Special American" describes Juan's problems of identity: "... the people in the street called him
'El Americano' ... 'Mexicano' among his family and friends"
(p. 5). "He knew he was not really a Mexicano" (p. 5).
"Christmas, Christmas" shows Rosa and Delia talking about
how people in other countries celebrate Christmas. "Chito's
Tree" is an insipid story that raises the question, "I thought
all Mexican people were Catholic" (p. 24). And "The Weeping Woman" is a story about two boys and the teacher's explanation of the legend of the Weeping Woman "as the mysterious Aztec goddess" (p. 45).

Victor, by Galbraith, simplifies a young boy's feelings
regarding his parents and school as a language problem:
"How would you like it if your mother could hardly speak
English ..." (p. 6). It describes the conflict between his
father's pride of Victor's "being manly" (p. 24) and the rules
against fighting at school. So mama goes to school to learn
to speak and read English, and Victor's problem is solved:
"Both parts of my life are coming together. My name is
Victor, and tonight I do feel like a winner" (p. 44). If only
the problems of self-identity were solved so easily and quick-
ly! The following Spanish words are misspelled: "llovan"
[sic] (p. 21 and p. 47), "Necesisto" [sic] (p. 24), and "caf
con leche" [sic] (p. 47).

We Are Chicano, by Blue, is the story of Carlos, a
12-year-old Mexican-American boy in Los Angeles. The
author discusses the problems of Mexican-Americans in the
U.S. in an insipid story by mentioning migrant workers,

city gangs, Mexican food, piñatas, and Mexican dances. An
example of the superficial understanding of a serious problem
is: "We are treated as the Indians were.... Pushed around
and pushed out by the Anglos" (p. 39). The story's advice:
"You know, Carlos, there are quiet heroes too" (p. 42).

Chicano Amigo, by Gee, is the story of an eight-
year-old Chicano boy, Kiki, with a big shining grin, whose
aim is to become a cub scout in spite of his lack of money
for a uniform and equipment. Kiki is trapped as a result of
a bad earthquake and is saved by Marc Conley, Kiki's reluc-
tant "amigo" and chief cub scout: "We amigos again, yes?"
(p. 96). Kiki's house: "Forget it.... He lives away over
by the dump" (p. 10). This is a shallow story with a feeble
hero that emphasizes Kiki's poor English, poverty, and eating beans.

Indian Paintbrush, by Chandler, explores Maria's
feelings about her Mexican father and Indian mother, as well
as the problems she encounters with other Indian girls in the
Sioux reservation: "If I talk in Spanish they make fun of
me" (p. 19). The story describes Indian customs and folklore and Maria's poverty: "Mamma had tried very hard to
stay in the Arizona town, working as a waitress, and doing
laundry for the families of the rich mine bosses" (p. 15).

Names and Places, edited by Julian Nava, is a collection of four uninspired stories about children's names,
Mexican food and sites in or near Mexico City.

Yucatan Monkey, by Beebe, is the story of a spider
monkey and his adventures in Yucatan. Through the monkey,
the reader encounters the fabulous wildlife and fruits of the
region. Unfortunately, at the beginning of the story the red
plate on the Chac Mool is explained as having "... one sinister purpose. Upon it, so archaeologists conjectured, the

still-beating hearts torn from human sacrifices were placed
as offerings" (p. 24).   Although the great Mayan history and
its achievements in mathematics and astronomy, its important writings, religion, and beliefs are later explored through
María and her uncle, I wonder if the reference to human
sacrifice at the beginning will not have a negative effect on
young readers.

      Little Dickens, Jaguar Cub, by Beebe, shows the de-
velopment of the close companionship between a jaguar cub
and John Barrett and their many adventures in the wild jun-
gle of Mexico's west coast.   There is a strong message of
the American hero who "... had outfought and slipped away
from bandits in northwest Mexico" (p. 13).   And, as the
protector of Mexico's archaeological findings, "John Barrett
remains the only man on the island and is charged with protecting it" (p. 122).   Mexicans are mentioned as plunderers
of their archaeological treasures (p. 108).

Stereotypes: Poverty

      To promote feelings of respect and appreciation to-
ward Mexican and Mexican-American values and customs,
the children must be made aware of the many stereotypes
prevalent in the books.

      Even though poverty is a reality in the lives of many
Mexicans or Mexican-Americans, students should realize
that not all Mexican or Mexican-Americans live in the extreme poverty that is portrayed in the books that describe
their lives.   The following are just a few of the many books
that show Mexicans or Mexican-Americans as either poor,
ignorant, dishonest, silly, or lazy.

      From Lupita's Hill, by Forsman, describes how poor

people live in Mexico: "... her small windowless room ..."
(p. 5). Lupita's sisters sleep on the ground "... onto the
mat ..." (p. 5). And Lupita wished "very much she could
give Mamacita and Papacito a real bed to sleep on ..." (p.
8). She felt embarrassed about her house: "It was poor,
ugly" (p. 16). In contrast, American girls are referred to
as rich on pages 34, 40, 151, and 191. Amy, a very intelligent, practical, American girl solves Lupita's problems.
The following are misspelled Spanish words or misused quo-
tation marks:

> "... caballo! Quieta!" (p. 25). [sic]
> "No te cayes!" (p. 62). [sic]
> "... protejeme!" (p. 74). [sic]
> "peónes." (p. 99) [sic]

Another book that shows a rich, honest, educated
American girl is But I Am Sara, by Means. It contrasts
Sara's family with Mexican servants and police, who are
shown as stubborn, dishonest, ignorant, and drunk. Sara's
father explains: "I can't promise it will always function ex-
actly as they do in the States ... Plumbing in Mexico--"
(p. 22). And, "The water is infected, the ground's infected,
so vegetables and fruits are, too" (p. 28). "And of course
giving him pesos encourages his begging" (p. 66). Sara
learned many things in Mexico, among which "Sara felt almost too shocked for thought. What had she expected of the
home of the very poor" (p. 144). The following words in
Spanish are misspelled:

"Piplio" [sic] (p. 64)   "usténd" [sic] (p. 75)
"pocito" [sic] (p. 106)   "lavendera" [sic] (p. 115)
"hablá" [sic] (p. 127)   "pan dulces" [sic] (p. 162)
"Perdóname" [sic] (p. 217)

Happy Days is a collection of four dull stories with

insipid characters and flat endings, edited by Julian Nava.
In "Medicine for Mother" Lupita has to sell her beautiful
hair to buy expensive medicine for mother.

The Chili Pepper Children, by Arnold, shows a silly
Mexican family that for a living raised and sold chili pep-
pers. Papa "... looked at his nine children. All were
barefoot like himself, standing in the sun near the adobe
mud wall of their home" (p. 28). And why would the family
not speak in Spanish? "Papa Pepper tried not to speak his
own Spanish language to his family" (p. 56). All the illustrations show barefooted Mexican peasants and men with
sombreros and ridiculous mustaches. The following words
in Spanish are misspelled:

> "¿Sabe ustedes?" [sic] (p. 73)
> "¿No es verdad, Carissimas?" [sic Spanish?]

Juan of "Parícutin" [sic], by Whitney, is the story
of Juan, a Mexican Indian boy, and his experiences upon the
birth of the Volcano. The geological descriptions of the volcano, lava, and earthquakes are very interestingly done; unfortunately, the author also emphasized detailed descriptions
of the Indians' poverty, superstitions and ignorance: "Juan
slept upon a petate on the floor of his little home in Parícutin" [sic] (p. 14). And mariachis: "They will get drunk,
and then they will roam the streets and play and sing all
night. A mariachi just can't stop singing" (p. 24). The
following words in Spanish are misspelled:

> "Coca, Cola, bien fio!" [sic] (p. 108)
> "Parícutin" [sic: Title page and throughout the
>   story]
> "Propina por Juan--por Macho" [sic] (p. 114)

Juan, by Stolz, also shows a poor Mexican boy, this
time in an impoverished orphanage in a small town. The

author does not understand Mexican habits or gay customs.
Mr. Radway states: "There is something about piñatas that
brings out the worst in people" (p. 111). As the children
are shown breaking a piñata and enjoying a picnic.

That's the Way It Is, Amigo, by Colman, describes
the poverty of Mexico in many ways: "... anything a Mexican could make or grow to earn a few pesos of the tourists"
(p. 6). "... the flimsy shacks that the poor Mexicans lived
in, with no plumbing, no electricity, and mats on the floor
for sleeping" (p. 7). "He wasn't about to take on the poverty of Mexico; it was too big and whatever you gave to the
beggars was like tossing coins into the sea ..." (p. 10).
The author also judges other Mexican traits: "In Mexico
people weren't in a hurry ..." (p. 6). "The old Mexican
machismo" (p. 33). "He made up his mind to take on the
easy-going Mexican ways, the mañana psychology" (p. 38).
"... when they drove they were maniacal, darting in and out
with utter disregard for any rules of the road" (p. 45).
Fortunately, David decides to return home.

Benito, by Bulla, is another story of a small orphan
boy who this time is taken into his uncle's house. There
he is expected to work very hard on the farm. His cousin
takes his only treasure, his crayons, from him. His uncle's
reply is, "You are poor, so you must work hard." Benito's
dream is to paint, and fortunately he meets the great artist,
Manuel Vargas, who is very kind and helpful to him.

The poverty and hardships of Mexican-Americans are
superficially described in Too Much Dog, by Forsee: "Mi-
grants work like burros" (p. 59); "But you do not know the
hardships of life as a migrant" (p. 84). And here are a
few psychological clichés: "He wished he'd get over finding
it so hard to talk to grown-up Anglos" (p. 78). "Papacito

hesitated to go where there are Anglo ways ..." (p. 188).
Cursory scenes of Mexican-American daily life and customs
and the great desire of a twelve-year-old boy to own a dog
are all there is to this story.

Basil in Mexico, by Titus, is an appealing mystery
told in a charming style. Basil, the Sherlock Holmes of the
Mouse World, is involved in solving the theft of the price-
less "Mousa Lisa" in Mexico City. Unfortunately, Mexico
is portrayed as a country with a cruel dictator, El Bruto
(The Brute), where "the crime rate is lower than ever before" (p. 25); and "those who pay the first price asked are
considered half-witted ..." (p. 49). For "authenticity" there
are also "Carmencita, a charming burro" (p. 93) and fiestas,
tacos, tortillas, and cheese enchiladas. The illustrations
depict mice as Mexican peasants with sandals, "sombreros,"
and "sarapes"; and as rebels with knives and guns. The
following words in Spanish are misspelled:

> "Plaza del Quesos" [sic] (p. 35)
> "Pilár" [sic] (pp. 41, 42, 50, and 62)

Stereotypes: Tortillas and Beans

A striking characteristic of Mexican food is its great
variety. Mexican and Mexican-American people enjoy many
colorful and delicious dishes cooked with extreme care. In
its preparation they use many different meats, fowl, fish,
sauces, vegetables, fruits, and/or cereals. Yet, in all of
the books about Mexican and Mexican-American people, they
are described as eating only "tortillas" and beans.

The Two Uncles of Pablo, by Behn, tells about nine-
year-old Pablo, who lives on a small, poor farm in the
mountains of Mexico with his peasant family. There are

several humorous incidents in which Pablo finally gets his
wish: a donkey (!). The family's supper is described:
"Maria is cooking tortillas and beans," (p. 12). And, "Often
they have had only a few beans to eat ..." (p. 12). The
black and white illustrations add to the "authenticity" of the
story: siesta time (p. 11), "metates and tortillas" (p. 11),
barefoot peasants, guitarras, sombreros, and poverty.

Chucho, the Boy with the Good Name, by Phillips, is
a long story about Chucho, an orphan Mixtec boy, who always helped people; he therefore received many kindnesses
from those he encountered in his journey to Huajuapan. The
village women provide him with his meals of "tortillas and
frijoles" (pp. 16 and 95). Chucho finally arrives with his
young brother and goat where he will "... learn to be a
weaver of hats as the men of her family, the Pachucas,
have been always" (p. 97). He was surprised to see electricity, as "... he had never thought of there being so many
lights" (p. 133).

The Place, by Elizabeth Coatsworth, describes Ellen,
the daughter of an American archaeologist, who has an exciting vacation in "exotic" Mexico. Jorge and Natividad
share with Ellen their secret about "the place," a magnificent, revered pre-Columbian cave that had beautiful frescoes,
ancient bowls, jars, parrots, doves, and jade beads. (The
illustrations on page 64 remind me of the Bonampak Murals.)
But the greatness of the Mayan civilization is never mentioned. This is a patronizing story of the clever American
tourists who condescend: "Perhaps Maria will give you each
a tortilla" (p. 11). And, the peasants "... weren't used to
forks, having always used their fingers" (p. 22).

Stereotypes: Siestas

Many of the books about Mexicans stress "siestas" and insist that all Mexican adults take a siesta every day. Students should realize that many Mexicans are hard-working people and that only in some small Mexican cities and villages where it gets very hot in the middle of the day and where there is no air conditioning, is taking a siesta necessary. Siestas are not common in big cities, where people are too busy working, or in towns where the weather is not oppressive. The following are just a few of the many books that emphasize siestas in Mexico:

Jose and the Mexican Jumping Bean, by Toepperwein, describes Jose, a typical Mexican mountain boy, the history of his town, Alamos, the characteristics of Mexican jumping beans, the annual harvest, summer days in Alamos, and the buying and selling of beans. It includes the typical dose of donkeys, tortillas, beans, and siestas: "The next day at noon, which is known as 'siesta time,' all places of business in Alamos were closed ..." (p. 9). The following words in Spanish are misspelled or misused:

> "Senor" [sic] (Throughout the book)
> "Entrar" [sic] (p. 27)
> "vivora" [sic] (p. 33)
> "Los Mananitos" [sic] (p. 36)

Tizz at the Fiesta, by Bialk, shows Tracy and her brother Don who go to Mexico on a short holiday. They meet their new Mexican friends, Carlos and Pepita, whose father owns a ranch. They learn about different Mexican and American customs; they go to the fiesta in Huejotzingo; they hear about donkeys, bullfights, and siestas: "Everyone in Mexico rests at siesta time, whether he wants to or not ..." (p. 40). And, this author states, obviously having be-

come an "expert" on Mexico after a short holiday there, that
Mexican children do not "... explore in the adventurous way
North American children like to explore" (p. 70).

Daisy, by Coatsworth, describes Mexico City and its
tourist attractions: bullfights--"Why, you haven't really been
in Mexico if you haven't seen a bullfight" (p. 17); piñatas,
burros, bandits, Aztec human sacrifices, tortillas, and
siestas--"It was siesta time, too early for the afternoon pro-
cession ..." (p. 25). There is an exciting incident in which
Daisy gets lost and is found by a blind singer, his wife, and
baby: "That night Daisy slept in a shed after a supper of
tortillas and black beans" (p. 39).

Stereotypes: Donkeys

Donkeys are constantly portrayed in books about Mexico: peasants are shown riding exclusively on donkeys, donkeys are used as background decorations of countless village
and town scenes, and donkeys are all Mexican boys' faithful
companions.   Although donkeys are truly part of the rural
life of Mexico, students should realize that they are not the
only means of transportation in Mexico, nor are they an indispensable aspect of Mexican life.   The following books illustrate how donkeys are used in numerous books about Mexico:

Carlos of Mexico, by Cavanna, has excellent black
and white photographs of Puerto Vallarta. "By Mexican
standards his [Carlos'] family was not poor. Carlos had
shoes to wear, a blanket with which to cover himself if the
nights grew cool, and plenty of tortillas to fill his stomach"
(p. 3).   What Carlos desired more than anything else in the
world was "A burro of his very own!" (p. 10).   So, we see

Carlos working to buy his own burro, women making tortillas, a children's Christmas party in a poor section of
Puerto Vallarta, and Carlos' new donkey with a broken leg.

Pizorro, by Vavra, has beautiful photographs in color
of Pizorro, a very poor Mexican peasant boy and his family
in their daily activities: "... tortillas and beans are what
the family eats every morning and evening" (unnumbered); at
the market; at a party breaking a piñata in which Pizorro
won "A burro to ride and to help me carry loads and to be
my friend!" (unnumbered). There are many photographs of
Pizorro with his burro in his village, with his aunt washing
clothes by the pond, in the main square, and at the church.

The Year of the Christmas Dragon, by Sawyer, is an
amusing story of the dragon that gave heat and light to the
people in a small Mexican village. The illustrations show
only sandaled Indians with sombreros, straw huts, and donkeys: "... every week Pepe drove his father's burro to
market ..." (p. 33). And several other stereotypes are included: "There were fiestas or special holidays almost
every week" (p. 31). "Mañana--tomorrow--was a hard-used
word in Mexico. It was the old custom here not to do today
what you could put off until tomorrow" (p. 61).

The Timid Ghost, by Brenner, is a story of a Mexican ghost, Teodoro, who is looking for the right person who
can answer just one simple question: "What would you do if
you had a sackful of gold?" There are many long, detailed
descriptions of the ghost's adventures with the ever-present
donkey: "... he gently appeared to a poor man who was
passing by with a burro" (unnumbered).

Stereotypes: Bullfighters

Several books emphasize the importance of bullfighting

in portraying the lives of Spanish or Mexican boys. Students
should realize that even though bullfighting is a popular pastime in Mexico and Spain, not every Mexican or Spanish boy
wants to become a bullfighter.

A Boy Named Paco, by Patiño, shows Paco, who
loves bulls and plays with all the boys; he is always the
"toro." He tries to get a job in a bakery and a fish market, but he is only interested in playing bulls. Paco runs
away and coincidentally lands a job where he can be the bull.
Although in this story the teacher is supposed to tell the
class "... all she could remember about Spain ..." (p. 1),
only bullfights are discussed.

Felipe the Bullfighter, by Vavra, has excellent color
photographs of bullfights, bulls, Spanish people, and Felipe
in his hometown of Los Palacios in southern Spain. Felipe,
who practices bullfighting in the courtyard of a poor section
of town, and at a ranch, gets ready for his first fight. The
people from all the neighboring ranches come to see him
fight and succeed.

The Village that Learned to Read, by Tarshis, describes the customs, problems and life in a small Mexican
village. Pedro's dream is to become a great bullfighter,
but ends up going to Mexico City looking for a big future in
shining shoes. The author mentions many serious problems
of Mexican people, such as food, housing, the high birth
rate, but she merely hints at the high illiteracy rate. Although the book was written in 1941, the problems are unfortunately still the same.

EVALUATION AND FOLLOW-UP ACTIVITIES

1. Ask the children to describe some of the problems of

acquiring a positive self-identity as experienced by Mexican or Mexican-American children. Some of the problems are:

a.   poverty

b.   rejection

c.   prejudice

d.   language difficulties

e.   lack of adequate models.

2.   Ask the children what Mexican children would like to become when they grow up, and to describe the daily life of a Mexican or Mexican-American grown-up. Hopefully, the children will not include stereotypes in describing the life of Mexican or Mexican-American people. (See Stereotypes under Outcomes.)

Grades: Seventh-High School

OUTCOMES

1. Describe the problems of self-identity as experienced by Mexican and Mexican-American young adults.

2. Describe the stereotype prevalent in the books about Mexicans and Mexican-Americans.

    a. Not all Mexicans or Mexican-Americans live in extreme poverty.

BOOKS*

Beatty, Patricia. The Bad Bell of San Salvador. William Morrow, 1973.

Binkley, Daisy R. The Isolation of Lupe. Naylor Company, 1974.

Bonham, Frank. The Vagabundos. Dutton, 1969.

Bonham, Frank. Viva Chicano. Dell, 1970.

Colman, Hila. Chicano Girl. William Morrow, 1973.

Hull, Eleanor. The Second Heart. Atheneum, 1973.

Johnson, Annabel and Edgar. The Last Knife. Simon and Schuster, 1971.

Jones, Thomas Firth. Rebel Gold. Westminster Press, 1975.

Means, Florence Crannell. Emmy and the Blue Door. Houghton Mifflin, 1959.

*Only books marked with an asterisk are recommended titles.

O'Dell, Scott.   Child of Fire.   Houghton Mifflin, 1974.

*Steinbeck, John.   The Pearl.   Viking Press, 1947.

DISCUSSION

Self-Identity

To promote feelings of respect and appreciation toward genuine Mexican and Mexican-American values and customs, students should be exposed to them, but regrettably,
at this time I am not aware of any fiction books** for young
adults that describe the varied and fascinating customs of
Mexican and Mexican-American people in a positive manner.
The following books stress only the negative aspects of their
personalities, such as corruption, and their language, social,
and economic problems.   One cannot help but wonder what
this abundance of negative characterizations does to the self-
identity of young Mexican-Americans.

Child of Fire, by O'Dell, is an adventure story that
includes cruelty, bullfighting, cockfighting, drugs, and Chicano gangs in which the Mexicans and Chicanos are the only
villains or young delinquents.   The worst of Mexico is emphasized, such as the practice of bribery and corruption:
"A big mordida.   But that was the way things worked south
of the border" (p. 7); Mexican-Americans are characterized
as emotional, resentful, thin-skinned, with an infantile sense
of honor, and "muy machos."

Viva Chicano, by Bonham, describes Keeny Duran and
his immature, selfish mother, who does not help, but ac-

_____
**See recommended titles listed under Books: Lifestyle and
Key Historical Developments, pp. 62, 63, 105, 106, 107.

tually is destructive to her children. The novel tries to
show understanding toward young people who grow up in emo-
tionally deprived homes, and the situations that are narrated
could be true about any "culture of poverty" family in any
big city in the world. The novel ends with Keeny deciding
to start a new life outside his home and the author's simple
solution to a most complex problem: "So why don't you
Chicano guys get involved in trying to clean the mess up?
Get in the Brown Berets, things like that" (p. 120).

The Vagabundos, by Bonham, describes the problems
of a wealthy American family in California. A retired father becomes restless because he has nothing to do. So the
father runs away and his son decides to follow him on a
boat to Baja California. The author ignores the fact that
educated Mexicans speak the Spanish language as well as
educated Americans speak the English language. There are
several insulting references to the Spanish language as spok-
en by uneducated Mexicans: "They'd need another interpreter
to put your border Spanish into Castilian" (p. 19). And,
"They had some good talks in border Spanish. It pleased
him that, after having Mexican help for years, his parents
still had to get him to translate sometimes. He had learned
Spanish as a child, from a succession of women named
Maria--Maria Guadalupe, Maria Estela, Maria Cruz" (p. 48).
The author also has negative comments on the Mexican personality: "Come on, Eric--when in Baja, do as the Mexicans do. Easy does it" (p. 107).

The Last Knife, by Johnson, tells the story of Howard, a young man who chose to go to jail instead of being
drafted. Through Howard's friends and their tales of con-
scientious objection, Rick is convinced that killing is not always good. One tale talks about Mexicans, but describes

them only in derogatory terms: "Especially Mexicans--
'those dirty wetbacks,' he called them. Rick never knew
why" (p. 66). And, about the mother in the story: "There
is no girlhood in the barrio--in Mexico City where she had
been passed from hand to hand for a few reales" (p. 78).

Chicano Girl, by Colman, is the superficial story of
a young girl and her poverty in a small town in Arizona.
The author describes Mexican customs as "... old fashioned
Mexican ways" (p. 15). To make the story more "genuine"
the author includes "piñatas," "tamales," and "rebozos."
And, she insists on the theme of poverty and ignorance of
the Mexican-American people: "It just seemed to me that
everything Mexican was poor, and why should we hang on to
that" (p. 128). The author condemns all Anglos and offers
a militant political solution to the injustices committed
against the Mexicans.

The Bad Bell of San Salvador, by Beatty, is the story
of Jacinto, a Comanche Indian boy who was captured and
raised in New Mexico during the 1800s. The boy served as
a servant in a very wealthy house in Santa Fe. There are
good descriptions of Santa Fe and the Santa Fe Trail as Jacinto and a group of New Mexicans go to settle in California.
Fiestas and cockfighting are interestingly described, but I
wonder about the need for judging Mexicans in statements
such as: "Cockfighting was like the Mexican tricks played
on horseback or with the reata. All foolish ... no, he could
not understand the Mexicans" (p. 130). "For a Ute you are
too small. There is no spirit in Mexicans" (p. 181). And,
describing an incident in the story: "More Mexican trickery"
(p. 156). "What sort of Mexican trickery was this?" (p.
165).

Stereotypes: Poverty

The only economic situation described in books for
young adults about Mexicans and Mexican-Americans is extreme poverty. Students should realize that even though
poverty is a reality in the lives of many Mexicans or Mexican-Americans, not all of them live in the hopeless poverty
that is described in the following books:

The Pearl, by Steinbeck, is a very well written short
novel that describes the terror, poverty, ignorance, and lack
of hope of the people of a small Mexican town. It tells
"... the story of the great pearl--how it was found and how
it was lost again. [It tells] ... of Kino, the fisherman, and
of his wife, Juana, and of the baby, Cayotito ..." (Preface,
unnumbered). All of Kino's dreams are centered on his son:
"My son will read and open the books ... he will know and
through him we will know" (p. 33). But unfortunately his life
does not include any happy moments.

Emmy and the Blue Door, by Means, tells a story
about Emmy Lane and her friends who decide to spend a summer in a remote Mexican village at a camp run by the
Friends (Quakers). They live in very primitive conditions
and so they try to understand the cultural differences and
abject poverty of the Otomi Indians in Central Mexico: "The
thing is, we can't imagine their standards of living until we
see them" (p. 54). "You ought to see some of this Mexican
water under a microscope" (p. 63). Emmy's romance with
Phil and his jealousies are the main plot lines through which
some negative aspects of Mexico are stressed: "With a
start Emmy realized the absence of those taverns so con-
spicuous in Mexico" (p. 127).

The Isolation of Lupe, by Binkley, is a soap opera

story of Guadalupe Salas' first romance, two marriages, and
two pregnancies. Weak characters and simplistic solutions
are described in "authentic" settings that include: beans,
siestas, "pulque," and wetbacks: "Those wetbacks don't know
how to break horses ..." (p. 66). Lupe finally becomes a
happy wife when she marries Mike O'Dell!

Rebel Gold, by Jones, is a novel that combines adventure with the exotic aspects of travel, drugs, and girls.
Mexico is always described as poor and dirty: "Mexico is
a country of poor people, of people in rags, of maimed and
halt and blind people ..." (p. 9); "... the Mexico of rags
and gutters?" (p. 11). And, Mexicans are portrayed as uneducated: "Like a Mexican, he ate without utensils, dipping
the tortillas into the mole ..." (p. 15). Mexico and Mexicans are stereotyped to produce a story about a "good"
American who decides to save the peasants from a rough
motorcycle gang that is only interested in obtaining mari-
juana.

The Second Heart, by Hull, is the story of a very
poor Mexican girl and her experiences as a servant and a
young teenager in an impoverished Mexican village. There
are good descriptions of Cuernavaca and its surroundings,
but the author generalizes and describes Mexicans from a
very limited perspective: "There was relief from that terrible village irritation of wondering where dinner was coming from--that fear that tortured the nerves and blackened
the mood, so that fathers and mothers hit whatever was near-
est and most helpless" (p. 139). And, "She, Marina, was
out of place for a thousand reasons, but they also could be
easily summed up: she was poor" (p. 181).

EVALUATION AND FOLLOW-UP ACTIVITIES

1. Ask the students to describe some of the problems of
   self-identity as experienced by Mexican and Mexican-
   American young adults.   The description should include
   the fact that a negative self-concept may result because
   in fiction books and other media Mexicans and Mexican-
   Americans are only depicted as cruel, violent, dishonest,
   "dirty wetbacks," who can't even speak English.

2. Ask the students what Mexican or Mexican-American
   young adults would like to become and to describe the
   daily life of a Mexican or Mexican-American adult.   The
   students should realize that not all Mexicans or Mexican-
   Americans live in extreme poverty.

Part 2

LIFESTYLES

Grades: Kindergarten-Second

OUTCOMES

1. Name the members of the extended Mexican family.

BOOKS*

*Balet, Jan. The Fence. Delacorte Press, 1969.

Brenner, Anita. A Hero by Mistake. William R. Scott, 1953.

Ets, Marie Hall. Bad Boy, Good Boy. Thomas Y. Crowell, 1967.

Ets, Marie Hall. Gilberto and the Wind. Viking Press, 1963.

Fern, Eugene. Pepito's Story. Farrar, Straus and Giroux, 1960.

*Flora, James. The Fabulous Firework Family. Harcourt, Brace, 1955.

Gaston, Susan. New Boots for Salvador. Ward Ritchie Press, 1972.

Ormsby, Virginia H. Twenty-One Children Plus Ten. Lippincott, 1971.

---

*Only books marked with an asterisk are recommended titles.

Ormsby, Virginia H.   What's Wrong with Julio?   Lippincott,
    1965.

Rhoads, Dorothy.   The Corn Grows Ripe.   Viking Press,
    1956.

Schweitzer, Byrd Baylor.   Amigo.   Collier, 1963.

DISCUSSION

Family

To develop an awareness of the similarities and differences between Mexican and American lifestyles, a view of
family life is essential.   The extended Mexican and Mexican-
American family is a constant source of support and encouragement to all its members.   Grandparents, aunts, uncles,
cousins, mother, father, brothers, and sisters--they all
have an important role in the life of a child and its affective
development.   Mexican children observe and feel from an
early age the affection and concern of all members of the
family toward each other, thereby creating a lifelong bond
of identity and love toward each member of the family.

Unfortunately, there are not many books that demonstrate the positive and creative force that the Mexican and
Mexican-American family is for the child.   Two better examples will be discussed first:

The Fabulous Firework Family, by Flora, shows a
family that for generations had worked together making fire-
works for their village.   The maestro, Pepito's father, was
commissioned to construct the finest firework castle to celebrate the birthday of the patron saint of their village.   The
story describes all the family at work in building the castle,
the actual day of the fiesta with the typical dancers dancing

the Moors and the Christians, the "toritos," and finally the
firing of the castle.   The castle was a success and Pepito
was very proud to belong to the Fabulous Firework Family.

The Fence, by Balet, compares the life, the homes,
and the attitudes of the very rich and very poor families in
Mexico.   Beautiful and colorful illustrations show the rich
family with its servants and luxuries, and the poor family
smelling the food from the rich family's kitchen and eating
bread.

There are many books that describe poor Mexican
families and stress only their negative characteristics:

Bad Boy, Good Boy, by Ets, is a shallow story of a
poor Mexican boy, Roberto, who always gets in trouble.   It
describes his problems with his father for stealing candy,
with his mother for waking his baby sister, and at the Child's
Center for throwing sand.   Roberto becomes "a good boy"
when he writes a short letter in English to his mother encouraging her to return home.   This story mistakenly stresses
the importance of the English language and belittles the sig-
nificance of family unity and their own language.

Twenty-One Children Plus Ten, by Ormsby, is a dull
story about Rosita and her Spanish-speaking friends, who do
not speak English.   The children are bussed to a new school
where "at first the new children did everything wrong ...,"
"... went the wrong way ...," "... sat at the wrong tables
...."   "They never do anything right!" (unnumbered).   Finally Rosita runs away.   Her mother brings her back the next
day and her new friends celebrate her "cumpleaños" [birth-
day] and "count in Spanish up to thirty-one," so, "... we're
glad to have thirty-one friends!"

What's Wrong with Julio, by Ormsby, shows the experiences of several children as they all learn English at

school, except Julio, who "... would not speak English."
"He's always bad. And he's always mad" (unnumbered).
All the children have a program for their parents, but no-
body comes to see Julio, who is not in the program. Julio
cries and all the children save money so that Julio can call
his parents by long distance. Julio is happy "... and he
spoke in English!" (unnumbered). The word in Spanish,
"Libraría [sic], is misspelled.

    The Corn Grows Ripe, by Rhoads, shows a very poor
family and its problems in Yucatan: the hardships of making
a very poor living out of growing corn; a daily diet of corn
and its many cooked uses; the superstitions and fears of uneducated people; their dependence on weather; the great infant mortality (Tigre, the boy in the story, lost his two
brothers in one week); the lack of knowledge of basic medi-
cinal practices, and their strong religious beliefs. Unfortunately, this is a realistic portrayal of the life of many Indian families in Mexico today.

    Amigo, by Schweitzer, is the story of an indigent
family and Francisco, the boy, who is very sad because he
wanted a dog to play with. But his father said, "No, Francisco. It's all we can do just trying to feed your brothers
and you" (p. 3). His mother suggests a prairie dog--because
it doesn't need food. The illustrations show a poor family
with basic needs.

    A Hero by Mistake, by Brenner, is the story of
Dionisio, a Mexican Indian who was always afraid. The author compares Dionisio's feelings to anybody else's feelings
of fear and bravery by telling the reader: "You know how
it is." Then, by mistake, Dionisio catches the town bandit
and becomes "the most intelligent and bravest man in the

whole region." The illustrations show scenes of life in the village.

The following are a few books that show Mexican children at play with the wind, with horses, or dancing:

Gilberto and the Wind, by Ets, is a poetic story of a Mexican boy who plays with the wind. The wind invites Gilberto to come out and play. They play with a balloon, and with the wash on the line. The wind breaks an umbrella, gives Gilberto a ride on the gate, and races Gilberto on the grass in the meadow. The wind does not like to fly Gilberto's kite, but it does blow a ripe apple from the tree and sails his boat. The wind blows Gilberto's pinwheel and soap bubbles, scatters the leaves, and breaks the trees. But Gilberto will not let the wind through the door.

New Boots for Salvador, by Gaston, has beautiful illustrations of a boy and horses in various activities: jumping, riding, trotting, or just standing. Salvador wishes to own a new pair of boots because he has "black rubber boots and a sad heart." "Salvador looked down at his rubber boots with dismay ... I have no boots" (unnumbered). Finally Salvador earns his boots.

Pepito's Story, by Fern, shows Pepito in the fishing town of Padingo. The children of Padingo swim, fish, and play in the woods, but Pepito only wants to dance. Estrellita, the daughter of the Lord Mayor of Padingo, is very lonely because her father doesn't want her to play with common children. She becomes ill and Pepito's gift to her is his dancing: "He knew that each one of us has something all his own to give to the world ... I'm glad I'm a dancer! I'm glad to be me!" (unnumbered).

EVALUATION AND FOLLOW-UP ACTIVITIES

1. Ask the children to name the following members of the
    extended Mexican family: father, mother, children,
    grandparents, aunts, uncles, cousins.

Grades: Third-Sixth

OUTCOMES

1. Describe the roles and importance of the father, mother, and other relatives in Mexican families.

2. Compare the extended Mexican family with the nuclear Anglo family.

3. Compare the differences between Mexican and Anglo children in expressing feelings and emotions.

4. Describe how a Mexican child would treat an adult.

BOOKS*

Alexander, Anne. Trouble on Treat Street. Atheneum, 1974.

*Clark, Ann Nolan. Paco's Miracle. Farrar, Straus, and Giroux, 1962.

Greene, Carla. Manuel Young, Mexican-American. Lantern Press, 1969.

Hazelton, Elizabeth Baldwin. Tides of Danger. Scribner, 1967.

*Krumgold, Joseph. ... and now Miguel. Crowell, 1953.

Martin, Patricia Miles. Trina. Abingdon Press, 1967.

*Nava, Julian, ed. A Traditional Voice in the Barrio. Aardvark, 1974.

Sommerfelt, Aimee. My Name Is Pablo. Criterion Books, 1965.

*Only books marked with an asterisk are recommended titles.

Stinetorf, Louise A. The Treasure of Tolmec. John Day, 1967.

*Stolz, Mary. The Dragons of the Queen. Harper and Row, 1969.

Taylor, Theodore. The Maldonado Miracle. Doubleday, 1962.

Van Der Veer, Judy. Long Trail for Francisco. Children's Press, 1974.

DISCUSSION

Family

To develop an awareness of the similarities and differences between Mexican and American lifestyles, a view of Mexican family life is essential. The extended Mexican and Mexican-American family is a constant source of support and encouragement to all its members. Grandparents, aunts, uncles, cousins, mother, father, brothers, and sisters--all have an important role in the life of a child and its affective development. Mexican children observe and feel from an early age the affection and concern of all members of the family toward each other, thereby creating a lifelong bond of identity and love toward each member of the family.

Unfortunately, there are not many books that demonstrate the positive and creative force that the Mexican and Mexican-American family is for the child.

The following are a few books that show positive aspects of Mexican and Mexican-American family life.

... and now Miguel, by Krumgold, gives a brilliant and human description of a boy and his family who own sheep in the mountains of New Mexico. The story describes Miguel's desire to go up the high mountain with the men who

tend the sheep and spend the whole summer there. Very
successfully the author describes the family life of Mexican-
Americans who live in the southwest: their customs, their
strong religious beliefs, their backgrounds, and their assim-
ilation into American society. But still the families maintain
their saints, holidays, food, and some of their language.

A Traditional Voice in the Barrio, edited by Nava,
has excellent black and white photographs describing the lifestyle of people who are still close to life in Mexico. Of
special interest are: "The Large Mexican Family," which
tells that "Abundant love is found in this big family because
each member is important to one another" (p. 16); "Mexican
Greetings," which describes Mexican salutations as "very ex-
travagant and expressive" (p. 21), and the importance of expressing "ourselves freely" (p. 21); "Mexican Brothers,"
which describes the intimacy and special feelings among
brothers in Mexican families; and "A Mexican Young Lady,"
which shows the importance for a well-bred señorita of learning the social graces and formal etiquette. There is also a
short section, "El Respeto Mexicano," which includes many
short sentences that illustrate the various meanings and sub-
tleties of that intense force, "Mexican respect": "Respect
is not had in riches, and riches cannot buy respect" (p. 79),
and "The children are taught to respect the parents from the
very start" (p. 79).

Manuel Young, Mexican-American, by Greene, shows
Manuel wishing to join Jimmy's baseball team and his lack
of skill in batting and pitching a ball. Through Manuel, Jimmy learns to appreciate and understand the lifestyle and history of Mexican-Americans. Also, Jimmy asks himself,
with embarrassment: "What will my friends think if I bring
a Mexican boy into the team?" (p. 40). The moral at the

end of the story is unsuccessfully developed in the plot:
"... it is even more fun to have some friends who are a little different. It takes many kinds of people to make a great
country like the United States of America" (p. 46).

Most of the books stress the hardships and humilia-
tions that Mexicans or Mexican-Americans experience in
their lives:

Tides of Danger, by Hazelton, is a suspense and adventure story centering on Trinidad Delgado, who tries to
find valuable pearls to replace the one that his brother stole.
He also wants to buy his family's freedom. (This concept
might mislead students into believing that there is slavery
in Mexico today. Poverty, yes; but slavery is forbidden by
the Mexican Constitution.) Other misconceptions about life
in Mexico are: "All of Mexico was harassed by robbers ..."
(p. 1). "... Don Gregorio had a right to separate a family,
to treat them like slaves ... it was wrong to be a bound
peon!" (p. 15). And, describing the Yaqui Indians: "They
are savage men, and once they begin ... The boy understands the minds of Indians" (p. 244).

Trina, by Martin, describes the life of a Mexican-
American family who live in a boxcar. There are many incidents that hold the reader's attention, such as Trina's desire for friends, her apprehensions about school, her joys
about a new hat and a new doll, and boys' tricks during Hal-
loween. But Trina's main concerns are her strong wish to
remain in the same town and her desire to learn to speak
and to read English. Unfortunately, the story gives the
Spanish language an inferior connotation: speaking to a ewe,
Trina says: "And to you it doesn't matter that I speak in
Spanish. You understand" (p. 17). And talking to her American friend, "'Buenos días,' Trina said. There it was,

Spanish again.   She felt her face grow hot" (p. 23).   The
following words in Spanish are misspelled or misused:

"debiera" (p. 32) [sic]   "Riense" (p. 56) [sic]
"ve" (p. 46) [sic]   "Esperánse" (p. 68) [sic]

Trouble on Treat Street, by Alexander, is the story
of the friendship between a Chicano boy and a black boy, and
involves violence and misunderstandings.   The author includes
several accepted racial stereotypes, poverty, and ignorance
among inner-city blacks and Chicanos, who finally develop a
true friendship and understanding.   The following Spanish
words are misspelled:

"Sentate" (p. 69) [sic]
"malesimo" (p. 104) [sic]

My Name Is Pablo, by Sommerfelt, describes with
realistic detail the hardships in Pablo's life: his parents expect him to work from a very early age, the police mistreat
him, and there is no institution that is interested in helping
him.   The author is very superficial in her criticisms of life
in Mexico City, describing only the negative side: "They
arrest you for such funny things in this country" (p. 10);
". . . but the police certainly are not the poor man's friends
in Mexico" (p. 11).   The author also censures Mexican
Christmas celebrations, the lack of causes to work for, and
Mexican people: "He knew, too, that revenge plays a part
in every Mexican's life, whether he has been in the Reforma-
tory or not" (p. 137).

The Treasure of Tolmec, by Stinetorf, describes the
sad life of the Tarascan Indians of Michoacán: "Since they,
and their fathers, had never known any other life, they took
it for granted that to be miserable was the common lot of a
'peon,' as the laborers in rural Mexico were called before

the revolution" (p. 14).   This is a mystery story which involves a boy, Jorge, and two evil men who wanted to steal
the only treasure of the village, a Titian painting.   Jorge
becomes a great hero only after suffering much humiliation
from the two evil men from the city.

Long Trail for Francisco, by Van Der Veer, is the
dismal life of Francisco and his three companions, who, as
illegal aliens, leave their families in a draught-stricken village in Mexico to seek their fortune in California.   The boys
smuggle themselves across the border, but Francisco's three
friends are captured by Immigration officers.   Francisco
finds life very difficult, barely keeping himself alive.   The
story emphasizes the dream of many poor Mexicans, con-
trasting it with life in the U.S.: "There were ... plenty of
jobs for Mexicans who like to work and earn money.... We
are poor here.   The little ones do not get enough to eat"
(p. 4).   "... handsome houses.   Where rich Americanos
live ..." (p. 25).

The Maldonado Miracle, by Taylor, is another story
of a twelve-year-old Mexican boy who entered the U.S. il-
legally to work in the fields.   It concludes with an interesting incident at a church, that many believed was a miracle.
The author insists in comparing life in the U.S. and Mexico
from a purely materialistic point of view: Jose's father
"... talked about the wonderful things he'd seen in California ... He'd talked on about having running water, an indoor
toilet, electricity, a TV set, a motorbike; maybe even a
car" (p. 29).   The author also denies any feelings of pride
or self-respect to Mexican people: "He told him everything
except the fact that he now thought he'd like to have white
skin and red hair like Miguel.   Speak English and live in a
house like that" (p. 87).   And, "Giron wore slacks, a yellow

jumper, and expensive-looking shoes.   Jose was proud to be
with him.   He looked more 'Americano' than Mexican" (p.
91).

Formality and Respect

Formality in manners and respect toward adults are
highly valued in Mexican and Mexican-American homes.   A
person may not be very wealthy, but if he or she displays
refined manners and treats all adults with courtesy, he or
she will be looked up to.   Money or success will never compensate for the lack of polite behavior or deference in treating adults.   The following are a few books that illustrate the
importance of formality and respect to Mexican and Mexican-
American people:

Paco's Miracle, by Clark, beautifully describes Spanish formal customs, marriage ceremonies, Christmas celebrations, shawls, and mantillas.   This is the story of an
old man and a young boy, Paco, who live in seclusion in the
mountains of northern New Mexico.   When the Old One falls
ill, Paco has to turn to the kind Spanish villagers in the valley below.   They willingly come and help Paco find a new
family and love.   Although the story repeatedly discusses
tortillas and donkeys: The Spaniards "... had come with
their burros and carts up the Royal Road from Mexico" (p.
15), and undervalues the French and Spanish languages:
"French and Spanish were easy ... English was the elegant
language, one he would like to learn perhaps, sometime" (p.
18), it does illustrate in an attractive writing style the theme
of kindness to all things.

The Dragons of the Queen, by Stolz, describes the
impressions of Mr. and Mrs. George Kenilworth from Boise,

Idaho, who have never traveled and decide to visit Mexico.
Their first impressions of the Mexican village are very negative: "It's a terrible town" (p. 9).   They are tired and impatient, as they have no place to spend the night.   Finally
the driver, Paco, suggests that they try to stay at the castle
with the queen and her seven dragons.   They spend a very
enjoyable evening dining and listening to the queen tell about
her life.   The queen dies that night, and the next morning
the Kenilworth's pedantic attitude toward Mexican people has
markedly improved.   The following Spanish words are misspelled:

> "senor and senora" [sic] throughout the story
> "Dona" [sic] throughout the story
> "esta" [sic] (p. 19) ["Usted" not included]

(See also discussion of A Traditional Voice in the Barrio, edited by Nava, especially, a "Mexican Young Lady" and
"El Respeto Mexicano," page 55.)

EVALUATION AND FOLLOW-UP ACTIVITIES

1.   Ask the children to describe the roles and importance of
     the members of the Mexican family.   The descriptions
     should include:

     Father: The provider of the family's financial needs.

     Mother: Main responsibility is the care of the house and
         children, but she is also able to be involved in other
         activities such as work or cultural projects, etc.

     Grandparents: Assist the mother in care of the children
         and the house.

     Aunts, Uncles and Cousins: Provide emotional and social
         support to all members of the family.

2.   Ask the children to compare the extended Mexican family

with the nuclear Anglo family.   The comparison should stress:

a.   That the extended Mexican family contains, besides the parents and children, grandparents, aunts, uncles and cousins; while the nuclear family is limited to the father, mother, and children.

b.   Many members of a Mexican family frequently get together for Sunday dinners, as well as birthday parties, weddings, and other major family and social events.

3.   Ask the children to compare the differences between Mexican and Anglo children in expressing feelings and emotions.   The comparison should indicate that:

a.   Mexican children are encouraged to express their feelings in public; such as, crying, kissing, shouting, etc.

b.   Anglo children are discouraged to express their feelings in public.

4.   Ask the children to describe how a Mexican child would treat an adult.   The description might include:

a.   That Mexican children should never address adults by their first names.

b.   That Mexican children should use proper manners and show respect at all times.

OUTCOMES

1. Describe the roles and importance of the father, mother, and other relatives in Mexican families.

2. Describe the effect of the extended family on Mexicans' loyalties.

3. Compare the differences in expressing feelings and emotions by Mexican and Anglo people.

4. Describe the importance of respect and formality in manners as taught in a Mexican household and used throughout a Mexican's life.

BOOKS*

*Anaya, Rudolfo A. Bless Me, Ultima. Tonatiuh International, 1972.

Colman, Hila. Friends and Strangers on Location. William Morrow, 1974.

*Coy, Harold. Chicano Roots Go Deep. Dodd, Mead and Company, 1975.

Dunnahoo, Terry. Who Cares About Espie Sanchez? E. P. Dutton, 1975.

Dunne, Marie Collins. Reach Out, Ricardo. Abelard-Schuman, 1971.

*Dwyer, Carlota Cardenas, editor. Chicano Voices. Houghton Mifflin, 1975.

---

*Only books marked with an asterisk are recommended titles.

Fairbairn, Ann. That Man Cartwright. Crown Publishers, 1970.

Fulle, Suzanne G. Lanterns for Fiesta. Macrae Smith, 1973.

*Galarza, Ernesto. Barrio Boy. University of Notre Dame Press, 1971.

Madison, Winifred. Maria Luisa. Lippincott, 1971.

Means, Florence Crannell. The House under the Hill. Houghton Mifflin, 1949.

Means, Florence Crannell. Us Maltbys. Houghton Mifflin, 1966.

*Roy, Cal. The Legend and the Storm. Farrar, Straus and Giroux, 1975.

*Vasquez, Richard. Chicano. Doubleday, 1970.

*Villarreal, Jose Antonio. Pocho. Doubleday, 1959.

Walden, Amelia Elizabeth. Same Scene Different Place. J. B. Lippincott, 1969.

Westheimer, David. The Olmec Head. Little, Brown and Company, 1974.

*Witton, Dorothy. Treasure of Acapulco. Julian Messner, 1963.

DISCUSSION

Family, Respect, and Formality

To develop an awareness of the similarities and differences between Mexican and American lifestyles, an understanding of Mexican family life, respect, and formality is essential. The extended Mexican and Mexican-American family is a constant source of support and encouragement to all its members. Grandparents, aunts, uncles, cousins, mother,

father, brothers, sisters--all have an important role in the
life of a child and its affective development. Mexican children observe and feel from an early age the affection and
concern of all members of the family toward each other,
thereby creating a lifelong bond of identity and love with each
member of the family.

Just as significant as the feelings of family loyalty
are formality in manners and respect toward adults as valued
in Mexican and Mexican-American homes. A person may not
be wealthy, but if he or she displays refined manners and
treats all adults with courtesy, he or she will be looked up
to. Money or success will never compensate for the lack of
polite behavior or deference in treating adults. The following books illustrate the closeness of Mexican families, and
the importance of formality in manners and respect to Mexican and Mexican-American people:

Barrio Boy, by Galarza, is a beautiful autobiography
that begins with descriptions of life in Jalcocotán, a mountain
village in the state of Nayarit, Mexico. Ernesto's family
was a poor, peasant, Mexican family that had excellent values
and manners. The author describes the philosophy and problems of pre-revolutionary Mexico and the difficulties, joys,
and sadness that his family experienced as they moved to
Sacramento. Ernesto emphasizes his mother's teachings:
"I was taught all the ceremonies of 'respeto'--the proper
greetings for delivering messages to the neighbors ... to
speak only when addressed... Breaches of these rules of
respeto fell somewhere between a sin and a crime. Not to
know them thoroughly and to observe then unfailingly showed
more than anything else that you were 'muy mal educado'"
[very poorly educated] (pp. 147-148). "Only children with a
bad education hurt people's sentiments ... I knew what she

meant by sentiment--a deep feeling of dignity and self-respect--that puzzling, powerful Mexican word, sentimiento" (p. 175). "In our family when I forgot my manners, my mother would ask me if I was turning pochito" (p. 207). Ernesto observes American manners: "... that the Americans do not ask permission to leave the room; that they had no respectful way of addressing an elderly person ..." (p. 236). The author describes his feelings after attending school in the U.S.: "At Lincoln, making us into Americans did not mean scrubbing away what made us originally foreign.... It was easy for me to feel that becoming a proud American; as she said we should, did not mean feeling ashamed of being a Mexican" (p. 211).

Bless Me, Ultima, by Anaya, is a very well written novel in which the author describes his early years in New Mexico and Ultima's influence upon his life. The important feeling of respect in a Mexican household is emphasized by the author's mother: "Oh, I would never have survived those hard years if it had not been for her--so show her respect. We are honored that she comes to live with us, understand?" (p. 7). And, "'¡Eugenio! Do not speak that way in front of Grande!' My mother was stern now. Not even the joy of having her sons back could break this rule of respect for the elders" (p. 173). Manners are also stressed: "Then she pulled Theresa forward and told her to greet la Grande. My mother beamed. Deborah's good manners surprised her, but they made her happy, because a family was judged by its manners" (p. 10). Unfortunately, the author's father drank excessively and, apparently, there was much crime and violence in his life, which are vividly narrated with large doses of profane Spanish words.

Chicano Roots Go Deep, by Coy, is a readable account

of Chicano history enriched with vivid examples of family
life, values, and customs. It describes the economic problems of Mexico and discusses the problem of wetbacks:
"... whose only crime, as one immigration official put it,
is being hungry ..." (p. 8). The chapter "Respeto, Orgullo,
Corazón and Idioma" (Respect, Pride, Heart and Language)
illustrates the differing concepts of values and respect.   Perhaps the author is overly optimistic when he states: "Scores
of poets have blossomed in the Chicano Renaissance ..." (p.
188), but he is authoritative in portraying the greatness of
Mexico during pre-Columbian and Colonial times. The author records Aztec achievements and graciousness and accurately states that the Aztecs "are remembered and much
blamed for cutting out the hearts of war prisoners on the
sacrificial stone" (p. 104).   This is a knowledgeable and
well-written history of the Chicanos, emphasizing the differences and the contributions of Mexicans and Mexican-Americans.

Chicano Voices, edited by Dwyer, is an anthology that
includes the major contemporary Chicano authors with brief
samples of their writings. Most of the selections describe
the living conditions of migrant workers; an example is The
Plum Plum Pickers by Raymond Barrio. Of special interest
are "When Women Speak," by Marta Cotera, which shows the
high position of Mexican women in the family structure and
the community (p. 101), and "The Organizer's Tale," by
César Chávez, which exemplifies Chávez's wisdom and hard
work in trying to form the farmworkers' union: "Before you
can run, you have to learn to walk" (p. 166).

Pocho, by Villarreal, is a very perceptive and well
written novel of a young man who grew up in California of
Mexican parents. Unfortunately, the author only describes

a Mexico of poverty and ignorance: "The ever-increasing
army of people swarmed across while the border remained
open, fleeing from squalor and oppression" (p. 16). And,
"We did not have the education because we came from the
poorest class of people in Mexico" (p. 61). And, again comparing the lifestyles of Mexican-Americans with the poor
people of Mexico: "We have certain rights in this country
.... It is not the primitive way here that it is in Mexico"
(p. 93).

Chicano, by Vasquez, is a novel, which traces through
several generations the tragedies and misfortunes of the Sandoval Family. The author describes the unfortunate conditions in which they lived in Mexico before the Revolution:
"Thousands, he knew, were fleeing either tyranny or poverty
in Mexico. To America" (p. 33). And then he relates their
early and difficult life in the U.S. as migrant agricultural
workers. The novel portrays many customs of uneducated
Mexican people, including a man's mistreating and beating
his wife, lack of manners or taste, heavy drinking, illiteracy or disrespect for education, urinating in public places,
etc. (Students should be reminded that this author is describing the lifestyle of the most uneducated Mexican people. Students should be cautioned against attributing this behavior to
all Mexicans or Mexican-Americans.) The author states that
burros are "Symbolic of the people of Mexico; they stood, ut-
terly defeated, without hope, resigned to whatever fate their
masters decided upon for them" (p. 357). This is a very
pessimistic novel about Mexicans and Mexican-Americans.

The Legend and the Storm, by Roy, presents through
the eyes of Rafa, a Mexican young man from a wealthy,
closely-knit family, a Mexico in conflict. The novel describes
complicated family relationships of aunts and uncles wrestling

for family power and control, but still striving for a united family (p. 52). It contrasts the living conditions of a wealthy family in Mexico City: their maids, cooks, home, etc., with the penury and lack of opportunities of Mexico's poor (p. 69). It condemns Mexico's political and legal customs: "You've come to a country without pity on a mission without hope. God himself has to bribe the lawyers and judges for justice here" (p. 16). And, "The Revolution of 1910.... Where does it exist? In fiction--novels and political slogans" (p. 82). The climax of the novel is Rafa's mental breakdown because of the massacre at Tlaltelolco on October 2, 1968, when his cousin and an unconfirmed number of students were killed.

Treasure of Acapulco, by Witton, is a very well-written story of drama and adventure by an author who truly knows life in Acapulco and its surrounding areas. Tony has to save two thousand pesos in three months; otherwise he has to leave his beloved Acapulco and live in Mexico City with his Uncle Juan. Tony's many difficult jobs and adventures with his American friend, Peter, are dangerous encounters: a violent boy, Lencho, starts a fight; Tony is attacked by a shark; Tony and Peter look for a buried treasure; and finally, Tony finds work on a fishing boat where he is very happy. As an exception, the beauty of life in Mexico City and Acapulco are very well portrayed, with nice friendships between Mexicans and Americans realistically described.

To avoid repeating myself incessantly, I have decided to discuss the following books as a group, because they all have one salient characteristic: they superficially describe Mexicans or Mexican-Americans as ignorant, unattractive, poor, drunkards, and with many more undesirable traits. The lifestyle that these books repeatedly emphasize presents a shallow and stereotyped view of the problems and aspirations of Mexican and Mexican-American people. The following books represent the opinions of ignorant authors who elaborate on their own misconceptions about Mexican or Mexican-American life without the true sensitivity of the artist or the insight of an educated human being:

Who Cares About Espie Sanchez? by Dunnahoo

Lanterns for Fiesta, by Fulle

The House Under the Hill and Us Maltbys, by Means

Same Scene, Different Place, by Walden

Reach Out, Ricardo, by Dunne

That Man Cartwright, by Fairbairn

Friends and Strangers on Location, by Colman

The Olmec Head, by Westheimer.

EVALUATION AND FOLLOW-UP ACTIVITIES

1. Ask the students to describe the roles and importance of the members of the Mexican family. The descriptions should include:

   Father: The provider of the family's financial needs.

   Mother: Main responsibility is the care of the house and children, but she is also able to be involved in other activities such as work or cultural projects, etc.

   Grandparents: Assist the mother in care of the children and the house.

   Aunts, Uncles and Cousins: Provide emotional and social support to all members of the family.

2. Ask the students to describe the effect of the extended family on Mexican loyalties. The description should stress that a Mexican feels a greater sense of loyalty to his family than to any other institution, i.e., church, or country.

3. Ask the students to compare the different ways Mexican and Anglo people express feelings and emotions. The comparison should include that:

   a. Mexican people are encouraged to express their feelings in public, such as, crying, kissing, shouting, etc.

   b. Anglo people are discouraged to express their feelings in public.

4. Ask the students to describe the importance of respect and formality in manners as taught in a Mexican household. The description should include:

   a. That from an early age children are taught to show respect to adults and use proper manners at all times.

   b. That in all social, educational and professional situations formal manners are expected to be followed.

Part 3

HEROES

OUTCOMES

1. Name two outstanding Mexicans or Mexican-Americans.

DISCUSSION

     Unfortunately, I do not know of any biography or auto-biography for the very young reader. Children may be interested in seeing pictures and hearing about the achievements of outstanding Mexicans, such as, Benito Juárez, Cuauhtémoc, Miguel Hidalgo, and prominent Mexican-Americans such as Ernesto Galarza, Joseph Montoya, and César Chávez.

     But Mexican-American children do need to increase their feelings of esteem for outstanding Mexicans or Mexican-Americans, so that they may feel a greater sense of identification with the personal goals or achievements of exemplary human beings.

EVALUATION AND FOLLOW-UP ACTIVITIES

1. Ask the children to name at least two outstanding Mexicans or Mexican-Americans.

OUTCOMES

1. Name three outstanding Mexicans and Mexican Americans.

2. Write a paragraph about the achievements of an outstanding Mexican or Mexican American.

BOOKS*

Axford, Roger W. Spanish-Speaking Heroes. Pendell Publishing Company, 1973.

Jackson, Robert B. Supermex; the Lee Trevino Story. Walck, 1973.

*Jacobs, W. J. Hernando Cortes. Franklin Watts, 1974.

*Johnson, William. Captain Cortes Conquers Mexico. Random House, 1960.

*Nava, Julian and Michelle Hall. Mexican American Profiles. Aardvark, 1974.

*Newlon, Clarke. Famous Mexican-Americans. Dodd, Mead and Company, 1972.

*Syme, Ronald. Francisco Coronado and the Seven Cities of Gold. Morrow, 1972.

*Syme, Ronald. Juárez, the Founder of Modern Mexico. Morrow, 1972.

*Syme, Ronald. Zapata, Mexican Rebel. Morrow, 1971.

*Treviño, Elizabeth Borton de. I, Juan de Pareja. Bell Books, 1965.

*Only books marked with an asterisk are recommended titles.

*Treviño, Elizabeth Borton de. Juárez Man of Law. Far-
rar, Straus and Giroux, 1974.

DISCUSSION

Mexican-American children need to increase their
feelings of esteem for outstanding Mexicans, Spaniards, and
Mexican-Americans so that they may feel a greater sense of
identification with the personal goals or achievements of exemplary human beings. In contrast to many of the fiction
books written about Mexicans or Mexican-Americans, most
biographies do not contain stereotypes and are generally
genuine descriptions of the lives of the people. The following books relate the lives of well-known artists, explorers,
philosophers, leaders, athletes, politicians, etc.

Famous Mexican-Americans, by Newlon, starts with
an introduction which discusses the Chicanos and their reasons for immigrating to the U.S.: "... the Mexican mestizo
came looking for bread" (p. 15). It then narrates the life
of distinguished Chicanos, with many sad illustrations of
discrimination in their difficult climb to success: Henry
Ramirez, Lee Trevino, César Chávez, Anthony Quinn, Ricardo Montalban, Henry B. Gonzalez, Joe Kapp, Jim Plunkett,
Joseph Montoya, Vikki Carr, Trini Lopez, Reies Tijerina,
Hilary Sandoval, Pancho Gonzalez, and Lupe Anguiano.

Mexican American Profiles, by Nava and Hall, is a
collection of the lives of twenty-six Mexican-American men and
women who were still alive at the time of the writing of
this book. It represents numerous occupations, life styles,
and political points of view. Each profile includes a black
and white photograph, three pages of information on major
themes and issues connected with each person, and questions

for discussion. Some of the people included are: Romana
Banuelos, Vikki Carr, César Chávez, Ernesto Galarza, Jim
Plunkett, and Reies Tijerina.

I, Juan de Pareja, by Treviño, is a beautiful story
which describes very well the Spanish court during the 17th
century. Through the life and work of the great Spanish
artist, Velasquez, we meet Murillo, Rubens, King Philip IV,
and Pope Innocent X. The life of Juan de Pareja, a Negro
slave, is illustrative of the sadness of many poor people in
Spain. I especially liked the admiration with which the author
describes Velasquez' art and personality. Also very realistically described is the importance of the Catholic Church in
Spain. This book offers many historical glimpses of Spanish
civilization and customs.

Hernando Cortes, by Jacobs, is an excellent visual
biography of Cortes. It is illustrated with authentic prints,
documents, and maps. It shows Cortes as a great military
leader, cunning politician, and daring adventurer who died
old, ill, and penniless. This is a magnificent history of
Cortes, the conquest of Mexico and Aztec emperors, lords
and common people. It also describes "the civilizations of
the ancient Maya--a people who built many roads, aqueducts,
bridges, and reservoirs of stone, and who had a calendar
more exact than any in use in Europe at the time ... they
had a well-developed system of writing and were expert in
science and mathematics" (p. 8).

Captain Cortes Conquers Mexico, by Johnson, is a
very well-written biography of Cortes, his time, and the important people at the time of the conquest of Mexico. Cortes' motives, his knowledge and understanding of people and
situations, and his courage are extremely well analyzed
throughout the book. "Montezuma" [sic], the superstitious

emperor of the Aztecs, is also understood and explained as
a product of his times. The author explains and describes
the importance of human sacrifice to the Aztecs. The Spaniards' interpretation of the new cultures they found is always
viewed in the light of their own religious prejudice: Cortes
says, "It is well to admire their arts, their fine buildings,
their wealth, and their music. But it is also well to remember the pyramids, where they make sacrifices to their heath-
en idols" (p. 106).

Francisco Coronado and the Seven Cities of Gold, by
Syme, describes the life of the Spanish explorer at the time
of the Conquest. Although the story is based on Coronado's
adventures in trying to find the legendary seven cities of
gold, it is also accurately critical of Spain's ambitions as a
conquering empire and its bad rulers: "They became am-
bitious and inclined to set themselves up as independent and
rebellious rulers in whatever country they had seized" (p.
38). And the reasons for Spain's interest in the New World:
"Trumpets were sounded, rich carpets unrolled, and distinguished honors made available only for those explorers
who returned with plundered treasure to fill the greedy cof-
fers of Spain" (p. 180). And, "... a host of grandees and
adventurers foolishly continued to drift across the mainland
in every direction in an endless search for nations to plunder
and mines to exploit" (p. 187). Coronado is described as
an exceptional, kind, mature ruler, who treated the Indians
as equals.

Juárez, Man of Law, by Treviño, is a simply written
biography that emphasizes Juárez' great personal attributes
and his dedication in setting up laws that guaranteed equal
rights to all men. Juárez' early life, marriage and exile,
the Reform Laws, the Maximilian problem, and the victory

of the Republic are interestingly described. It also deals
honestly with Mexico's problems of misery and ignorance.

Juárez, the Founder of Modern Mexico, by Syme, is
another very well-written biography of one of Mexico's greatest presidents. I definitely agree with the author when he
states: "Even those Mexicans who had been shocked by Maximilian's personal tragedy grudgingly admired Juárez for his
courage and perseverance, his faith and integrity. In the
entire history of Mexico no man had ever enjoyed a comparable record" (p. 169). The author shows great understanding in describing the problems of Mexico: the unlimited
personal ambition and greed of its politicians, the great
power of the church that controlled and subjected the minds
of the people, the mishandling of its natural resources, and
the political interference of the great European and American
powers.

Zapata, Mexican Rebel, by Syme, gives the reader an
overview of Zapata's life and also describes important events
of the Mexican Revolution. It presents somber facts about
Mexico: "The Mexican Indians numbered ten million in a
total population of about twelve million.... Eighty per cent
of them were illiterate and living in great poverty" (p. 14
and 16). It also discusses other leaders of the Mexican
Revolution: "Madero was one of those politicians who have
admirably sound ideas before they attain a position of power.
But once in power they fear to risk their popularity with a
wealthy minority by enacting urgently needed reforms. Madero completely lost his nerve and carried on in the tradi-
tion of Diaz" (p. 35-36).

Supermex; the Lee Trevino Story, by Jackson, is a
biography of the famous Mexican-American golfer which con-
centrates on his professional career. But I wonder about the

need for the following generalizations: "Speaking of his great
financial success, Lee once remarked, 'You can call me a
Spaniard now, because who ever heard of a rich Mexican?'"
(p. 13); "Like blacks, Mexican-Americans usually lead hard
lives in severe poverty ... the majority are unskilled laborers or farm workers ..." (p. 9). And, "... comparing the
blond, blue-eyed, college-educated Jack Nicklaus with Lee,
a hustling, happy-go-lucky Chicano dropout" (pp. 52-53).

    <u>Spanish-Speaking Heroes,</u> by Axford, is a collection
of twenty-three biographical sketches which illustrate the suc-
cesses of Spanish-speaking immigrants or children of immigrants. The author emphasizes the positive contributions and
the personal accomplishments in their lives. Unfortunately,
the three-page sketches of each person offer only encyclopedic
information and are not interestingly written. Some of the
people mentioned are: Alfonso Ramon Lopez, César Chávez,
Trini Lopez, Pablo Casals, Roberto Walker Clemente,
Joseph Montoya, Ricardo Montalban, Jim Plunkett, and Lee
Trevino.

EVALUATION AND FOLLOW-UP ACTIVITIES

1.   Ask the students to name at least three outstanding Mexi-
    cans or Mexican-Americans.

2.   Ask the students to write a paragraph about the achieve-
    ments of an outstanding Mexican or Mexican-American.

OUTCOMES

1. To be able to identify and describe the major contributions and/or activities of at least three outstanding Mexican or Mexican-American presidents, political leaders, writers, artists, athletes, etc.

2. To describe the impact of at least one of the following men on the ideals of Mexican and Mexican-American youth:

Emiliano Zapata   César Chávez
Benito Juárez   Francisco Villa

BOOKS*

*Galarza, Ernesto. Barrio Boy. University of Notre Dame Press, 1971.

*Noble, Iris. Spain's Golden Queen Isabella. Julian Messner, 1969.

*Rouverol, Jean. Pancho Villa. Doubleday, 1972.

DISCUSSION

Mexican-American students need to increase their feelings of esteem for outstanding Mexicans, Spaniards, and Mexican-Americans, so that they may feel a greater sense of identification with the personal goals or accomplishments

*Books marked with an asterisk are recommended titles. (See also Books listed under Heroes, Grades: Third-Sixth, pp. 72 and 73.)

of exemplary human beings. In contrast to many of the fiction books written about Mexicans or Mexican-Americans,
most biographies do not contain many stereotypes and are
generally genuine descriptions of the lives of the people.

Pancho Villa, by Rouverol, is an excellent biography
of a very controversial Mexican historical figure. The author states many truths that are certainly omitted in Mexican
history books: the ruthless ambition of many Mexican leaders and their continual exploitation and abuse of their political
strength for personal profit; the great influence of U.S. am-
bassadors and presidents in Mexican politics; the great and
uncontrolled power of the Catholic Church in Mexico; and the
impoverished conditions and abuse of the great majority
of the Mexican people. The author honestly describes the illiteracy and hardships of Villa's life--she writes about a violent man with many weaknesses and strengths who was a
product of his times and circumstances. The author is also
very critical in describing many of the cherished "heroes" of
the Mexican Revolution.

Spain's Golden Queen Isabella, by Noble, is an outstanding biography of Queen Isabella of Castille, with glimpses
of life in Spain during the 15th century: the Muslim Empire
and its advances in learning; Henry IV and his corrupt court;
Torquemada's hatred of the Jews; Ferdinand's unfaithfulness
to the Queen and his illegitimate children; the beginnings and
horrors of the Inquisition: "The harm it did to Spanish
Christians did not show itself so plainly on the surface; un-
derneath it would become a deep, running sore in the body of
Spain" (p. 95); the Queen's support of Columbus' trip to the
Indies; the reconquest of Granada from the Moors; the suffer-
ings of the Jews after the expulsion; and Isabella's achievements in Spain: "peace and order, law and justice, culture,

hospitals, schools and churches" (p. 156). The author states
that after the Queen died in 1504, "The Golden Age of Spain
was over" (p. 179), and that "Unfortunately, none of those
who followed immediately after her were like her; they left
Spain plundered, misruled and weak" (p. 181).

(See discussion of Barrio Boy, by Galarza, under
Lifestyle, Grades: Seventh-High School, pp. 64 and 65.)

EVALUATION AND FOLLOW-UP ACTIVITIES

1. Ask the students to identify and describe the major contributions and/or activities of at least three outstanding
   Mexican or Mexican-American presidents, political leaders, writers, artists, athletes, etc.

2. Ask the students to describe the impact of at least one
   of the following men on the ideals of Mexican and Mexican-American youth. The description might include:

   Zapata: The right of every Mexican peasant to cultivate
   his own land.

   Juárez: Separation of Church and State.

   Chávez: Rights of the farm workers.

   Villa: Rights of the Mexican peasants.

Part 4

FOLKLORE

Grades: Kindergarten-Second

OUTCOMES

1. Appreciation of the beauty and variety of Mexican folk-lore.

2. Children will be able to contrast the lifestyles of the very rich and the very poor.

3. Children will be able to act out and describe a folktale that illustrates the wit and cleverness of Mexican people.

BOOKS*

*Flora, James. The Fabulous Firework Family. Harcourt Brace, 1955.

*Lyons, Grant. Tales the People Tell in Mexico. Messner, 1972.

Politi, Leo. Song of the Swallows. Scribners, 1949.

DISCUSSION

There is a great beauty and variety in Mexican folk-lore that children can easily appreciate and enjoy. Folk

---

*Only books marked with an asterisk are recommended titles.

tales, folk arts, folk dances, and folk songs give children
delight and new insights into the colorfulness, gaiety, spontaneity, and genuine artistic talents of the Mexican people.

Tales the People Tell in Mexico, by Lyons, is a collection of popular tales that show the wit, wisdom, and flavor of Mexico. Included are animal tales and tales that portray the life of the very rich in Mexico. In "Ashes for
Sale" the hero makes a lot of money and: "He lost no time
enjoying his new riches" (p. 79). There is also an excellent
selection of Mexican sayings.

(See Discussion of The Fabulous Firework Family, by
Flora, under Lifestyle, Grades: Kindergarten-Second, pp. 48
and 49. This story describes with excellent illustrations a
unique Mexican folk art: firework castles.)

Song of the Swallows, by Politi, uses the setting of
a California mission to tell a beautiful story about swallows.
Attractive illustrations show the mission, the garden, and
Juan learning about swallows and how to take care of his
own garden. It is unfortunate, however, that the meaning
and words of a very traditional Mexican song were changed
from a very sad song of farewell that every Mexican knows,
to a happy song of swallows. The author described the mission in a very authentic historical setting. Why not keep
Mexican traditions as Mexicans know them?

EVALUATION AND FOLLOW-UP ACTIVITIES

1.   Ask the children to express their feelings about a sample
     of Mexican folklore.

2.   Ask the children to contrast the lifestyles of the very
     rich and the very poor.

3.   Ask the children to act out and describe a folktale that
     illustrates the wit and cleverness of Mexican people.

Grades: Third-Sixth

OUTCOMES

1. Appreciation of the beauty and variety of Mexican folk-lore.

2. Students will be able to contrast the lifestyles of the very rich and the very poor.

3. Students will be able to give examples from the tales that show how the folktales:

    a. Keep alive ancient events and traditions;

    b. Rationalize and sanction conduct;

    c. Amuse.

BOOKS*

*Brenner, Anita. The Boy Who Could Do Anything and Other Mexican Folk Tales. Young Scott Books, 1970.

Comins, Jeremy. Latin American Crafts and Their Cultural Backgrounds. Lothrop, Lee and Shepard, 1974.

Lindsey, Davie L. The Wonderful Chirrionera and Other Tales from Mexican Folklore. Heidelberg Publishers, 1974.

*Parish, Helen Rand. Our Lady of Guadalupe. Viking Press, 1955.

Ross, Patricia Fent. In Mexico They Say. Knopf, 1942.

*Only books marked with an asterisk are recommended titles. (See also Books listed under Folklore, Grades: Kindergarten-Second, page 81.)

DISCUSSION

There is a great beauty and variety in Mexican folklore that children can easily appreciate and enjoy. Folk
tales, folk arts, folk dances, and folk singers may give children delight and new insights into the colorfulness, wit,
gaiety, spontaneity, and genuine artistic talents of the Mexican people.

Although folk tales can be used to keep alive ancient
events and traditions, and to rationalize and sanction conduct,
children should first be amused by hearing or reading the
tales.

Unfortunately, very few of the following books maintain the original flavor of Mexican tales. Several seem to
be tourist-type adaptations for American children of well-
known stereotypes of Mexican people:

The Boy Who Could Do Anything and Other Mexican
Folktales, by Brenner, is an outstanding collection of twenty-
six short, authentic folktales that are simply written. The
delightful tales "The Boy Who Took Care of the Pigs" and
"The Magic Grocery Store" will amuse all children by telling
about the poor boy who became rich (a popular theme in
Mexican folktales). A few examples of folk tales that keep
alive ancient events and traditions are: "Malintzin" (p. 125),
which talks about the controversial heroine who helped Cortes
conquer Mexico; "Teutli, the Mountain That Is Alive" (p. 23),
which shows an Aztec emperor protecting his people from
trains and inventions; and "The Bow, the Deer, and the Talking Bird" (p. 90), which describes a rich Aztec merchant
who leaves three fortunes to his three sons. Three examples
of folk tales that rationalize and sanction conduct are: "The
Dead Man Who Was Alive" (p. 96), which tells how people

explained Pedro's unusual behavior by saying "that he was crazy"; "Some Impatient Mule-Drivers" (p. 21), which shows "that people who think they are clever are sometimes mistaken" (p. 22), as the mule-drivers lose their salt, their money, and their mules; and "Funny, Funny" (p. 52), which tells the story of Felipe, who never did any work, but when he married Pancho's daughter "he turned out to be a good son-in-law after all" (p. 58).

Our Lady of Guadalupe, by Parish, is a beautifully written story of a very popular tradition-legend of all Catholics of Mexico. The author tells the story of Our Lady of Guadalupe in a very real 16th-century setting in Mexico. She describes the living conditions of the Indians at the time of the Conquest, the power of the Catholic Church over the Indians, the force of the Inquisition; and finally she tells how the Virgin appeared to Juan Diego, the humble Indian, and how she instructed him to go to the Bishop. This miracle-legend is widely believed by Catholics in Latin America. The author certainly captures the feeling of respect toward the Church and even intermixes some Nahuatl words with her text.

Latin American Crafts and Their Cultural Backgrounds, by Comins, has attractive black and white photographs and drawings of gold masks, stone sculptures, clay pottery, and wool and cotton picture weavings of Latin American folk art. It gives detailed how-to instructions on crafts in the style of both ancient and modern Latin America using easy-to-find materials. This book is especially valuable for students who are interested in crafts, but not for those whose interest is in Latin American folk arts.

In Mexico They Say, by Ross, is a collection of fourteen adaptations of Mexican legends of pre-Columbian and

Colonial themes. Only a few of the tales have maintained
their originality. They are: "The Million-Dollar Somer-
saults," which shows the life of the very rich in Mexico City
with attractive illustrations, and "The Smoking Mountain,"
which is the popular legend of Ixtlaccihuatl's and Popocatepetl's
great love. Unfortunately, in the other folktales the author
elaborates on her own misconceptions. Some samples of her
misunderstandings are the following statements: "... the Indians worshipped strange gods of whom they made stone
idols" (p. 151). (Strange to whom? What is she implying?)
And, "Now the animal people of the forest had been very happy since the Tarascans had the Christian religion, for that
meant that none of them was sacrificed to the old gods any
more" (p. 168). (Why stress the relationship between human sacrifice and the Tarascan religion? Can she demonstrate the superiority of the Christian religion?) The illustrations are also degrading, as they show typical barefoot
Indians, sombreros, and donkeys.

The Wonderful Chirrionera and Other Tales from Mexican Folklore, by Lindsey, is a collection of adapted Mexican folktales with unbecoming, stereotypical illustrations
which unfortunately portray Mexicans as bandits, riding on
donkeys, wearing sombreros, and sleeping on a cart. "The
Wonderful Chirrionera" has been rewritten for children to
reinforce their misconceptions of Mexican people. Juan Santos, a poor mule herder who worked hard every day, often
only to spend all his hard-earned and scanty wages on tequila Saturday night, so that some days there were "neither
tortillas nor frijoles in the house" (unnumbered). "Siestas,"
"burros," "much tequila drinking," "mustache to droop over
his mouth," and "sarapes to pull over his ears" are distor-
tions that misrepresent Mexican people and their folktales.

The other tales in this collection are better adapted and may be used to amuse children.   In the following two tales the popular Mexican theme of the poor man who became rich is used: "Charge This to the Hat" tells of a poor, simple farmer who devises an ingenious way to gain revenge on his snobbish, wealthy neighbor and becomes a rich man for his efforts.   "Sandal Leather" describes a poor man who believed what everyone told him, but in the end gets a fortune in gold and plays a trick on the town's wealthy farmer. "Three Bits of Advice" shows a stubborn boy deciding to heed the good advice of a wise old stranger.

EVALUATION AND FOLLOW-UP ACTIVITIES

1. Ask the students to express their feelings about a sample of Mexican folklore.

2. Ask the students to contrast the lifestyles of the very rich and the very poor.

3. Ask the students to give at least one example of folk tales that:

    a.   Keep alive ancient events and traditions

    b.   Rationalize and sanction conduct

    c.   Amuse.

Grades: Seventh-High School

OUTCOMES

1. Appreciation of the beauty and variety of Mexican folklore.

2. Students will be able to contrast the lifestyles of the very rich and the very poor.

3. Students will be able to give examples from the tales that show how the folktales:

   a. Keep alive ancient events and traditions

   b. Rationalize and sanction conduct

   c. Amuse.

BOOKS*

Braddy, Haldeen. Mexico and the Old Southwest. National University Publications, 1971.

*Paredes, Américo, editor. Folktales of Mexico. University of Chicago Press, 1970.

*Robe, Stanley, editor. Antología del Saber Popular. University of California, 1971.

*Toor, Frances. A Treasury of Mexican Folkways. Crown Publishers, 1947.

DISCUSSION

There is a great beauty and variety in Mexican folk-

*Only books marked with an asterisk are recommended titles.

lore that students can easily appreciate and enjoy. Folk
tales, folk arts, folk dances, and folk songs may give students delight and new insights into the colorfulness, wit,
gaiety, spontaneity, and genuine artistic talents of the Mexican people.

Although folk tales can be used to keep alive ancient
events and traditions, and to rationalize and sanction conduct,
students should first be amused by hearing or reading the
tales. Besides the books discussed in this section, students
may also enjoy some of the folk tales recommended for
younger readers which demonstrate the flavor, wit, and wisdom of Mexican people.

Folktales of Mexico, edited by Américo Paredes, is
an excellent scholarly collection of Mexican folklore with an
authoritative foreword and introduction. This book contains
many folk tales for the student who is interested in studying
and selecting Mexican tales. Unfortunately, because Paredes
tried "to achieve the style of each narrator," many of the
tales are confusing and difficult to understand. The excellent Index of Motifs can be very helpful in selecting tales
that amuse, that keep alive ancient events and traditions, and
that rationalize and sanction conduct. Part I includes Legendary Narratives with an abundance of historical and religious
legends. "Mal de Ojo" (p. 32) and " ¡Qué Veo!" (p. 33)
are two short, very well-known tales. Part II consists of
Animal Tales, and Part III of Ordinary Tales (wonder and
adventure tales), of which "Blancaflor" (p. 78) is a well-told
love story of a magic horse. These tales are the easiest to
understand. Part IV, Jokes and Anecdotes, includes religious
and political jokes and jokes about everyday life. Part V is
a collection of Formula Tales.

A Treasury of Mexican Folkways, by Toor, is an outstanding account of the customs, folklore, traditions, beliefs, fiestas, dances, and songs of the Mexican people. It contains useful background information with interesting, short descriptions of various aspects of Mexican folkways.

Antología del Saber Popular, edited by Robe, is a collection of oral folk material written in colloquial Spanish. (A good knowledge of Spanish is necessary to get the flavor of the folk tales.) The Table of Contents may be used to select tales for different purposes or occasions. It includes folk tales, jests and anecdotes, legends and beliefs, popular medicine, prayers, verses, children's games and lullabies, pastorela, riddles, proverbs and customs.

Mexico and the Old Southwest, by Braddy, is a result of all of the author's publications about folklore. There is a little bit of everything: the vanished glories of the West and its people; international smugglers, heroin pushers and drug addicts; the lingo of the cowboy; political assassinations during the Mexican Revolution; Pancho Villa, "the hombre of many faces"; La Nacha, the empress of the narcotics underworld; and Cockfighting, its history and present-day practices in Mexico. The book lacks continuity and its use as a reference source is limited because it does not have an index.

EVALUATION AND FOLLOW-UP ACTIVITIES

1. Ask the students to express their feelings about a sample of Mexican folklore.

2. Ask the students to contrast the lifestyles of the very rich and the very poor.

3. Ask the students to give at least one example of folk tales that:

    a.   Keep alive ancient events and traditions

    b.   Rationalize and sanction conduct

    c.   Amuse.

Part 5

KEY HISTORICAL DEVELOPMENTS
Leading to Present Mexican-American Culture

Grades: Kindergarten-Second

OUTCOMES

1. To name as pre-Columbian or modern, pictures of Mexican architecture, art, and painted books (códices).

2. To expose the children to some outstanding samples of pre-Columbian temples, religious objects, ornaments, jewelry, and painted books (códices).

BOOKS*

*Glubok, Shirley. The Art of Ancient Mexico. Harper, 1968.

*Glubok, Shirley. The Art of the Spanish in the United States and Puerto Rico. Macmillan, 1972.

DISCUSSION

Mexican-American children should be proud of the great heritage that is legitimately theirs. Through an early exposure to the marvelous richness of pre-Columbian, Spanish, Mexican, and Mexican-American cultures, children may develop the genuine self-respect that only comes from a true

---

*Books marked with an asterisk are recommended titles.

understanding of one's own history and background.

For the young child, perhaps just an introduction to the arts of pre-Columbian, Spanish, Mexican, and Mexican-American people is necessary to awaken a lifelong appreciation and interest.   Any attractive art or architecture book of the above mentioned cultures will serve this purpose.   The following are only two of the many outstanding art books that can be used with young children:

The Art of Ancient Mexico, by Glubok, has excellent photographs of the temples, religious objects, decorative ornaments, jewelry, weapons and painted books (códices) of most of the great pre-Columbian cultures, with the exception of the Mayas.   The Aztec, Mixtec, Toltec, Olmec, and Zapotec civilizations are represented with simple descriptions that highlight their outstanding achievements before the arrival of the Spaniards in Mexico.

The Art of the Spanish in the United States and Puerto Rico, by Glubok, is shown in this collection of black and white photographs of Spanish homes, churches, missions, forts, furniture, wall-hangings, blankets, tinware, and carved or painted holy images.   This book can be used as a brief introduction to art with a Spanish influence.

EVALUATION AND FOLLOW-UP ACTIVITIES

1.   Ask the children to name at least two pre-Columbian and two modern pictures of Mexican architecture, art, and painted books (códices).

2.   Ask the children to express their feelings about some outstanding samples of pre-Columbian temples, religious objects, ornaments, jewelry, and painted books (códices).

Grades: Third-Sixth

OUTCOMES

1. Describe reasons for Spanish colonial expansion.

2. Pre-Columbian Mexico: describe achievements of Mayan, Teotihuacan, Toltec, Mixtec-Zapotec and Aztec cultures. Draw a picture of your favorite pre-Columbian design, pyramid, sculpture, etc.

3. Colonial Mexico--fusion of two cultures: identify characteristics in architecture, lifestyle, and customs which illustrate the fusion of the Spanish with the pre-Columbian cultures.

4. Mexican-American conflict: describe the political situation in Mexico and the U.S. prior to the War, the upheavals that occurred during the War, and the major results of the War.

5. Mexican-Americans today:

    a. Describe the economic and social problems of Mexico today.

    b. Describe why poverty is the main reason for immigration to the U.S.

    c. Describe the results of immigration.

BOOKS*

*Acuña, Rudolph. The Story of the Mexican Americans. American Book Company, 1969.

Caldwell, John C. Let's Visit Mexico. John Day, 1965.

*Only books marked with an asterisk are recommended titles.

Coleman, Eleanor S. The Cross and the Sword of Cortes.
Simon and Schuster, 1968.

Darbois, Dominique. Tacho Boy of Mexico. Follett, 1961.

*Gómez, Barbara. Getting to Know Mexico. Coward-Mc-
Cann, 1968.

McNeer, May. The Mexican Story. Ariel Books, 1953.

*Martinez, Gilbert and Jan Edwards. The Mexican American.
Houghton Mifflin, 1973.

Molnar, Joe. Graciela--a Mexican-American Child Tells
Her Story. Franklin Watts, 1972.

O'Dell, Scott. The Treasure of Topo-el-Bambo. Houghton
Mifflin, 1972.

*Ross, Patricia Fent. Mexico. Fideler Company, 1962.

Swiger, Elinor Porter. Mexico for Kids. Bobbs-Merrill,
1972.

*Tebbel, John and Ramon Edwardo Ruiz. South by Southwest.
Doubleday, 1969.

*Treviño, Elizabeth Borton de. Here Is Mexico. Farrar,
Straus and Giroux, 1970.

*Treviño, Elizabeth Borton. Nacar, the White Deer. Far-
rar, Straus and Giroux, 1963.

Weiner, Sandra. Small Hands, Big Hands. Pantheon
Books, 1970.

DISCUSSION

Mexican-American children should be proud of the
great heritage that is legitimately theirs. Through an understanding of the marvelous richness of pre-Columbian, Spanish, Mexican and Mexican-American cultures, children may
develop the genuine self-respect that only comes from a true

knowledge of one's own history and background.

Books on art and architecture and biographies (see books listed under "Heroes") of the men and women of the different historical periods of Spain, Mexico, and the Southwest may be used in addition to the following books, which are discussed in chronological historical order:

Colonial Mexico

The Cross and the Sword of Cortes, by Coleman, is a historical account of the conquest of Mexico through the narration of the priest Aquilar, who was a great admirer of Cortes and Malinche. Cortes is described as a courageous and intelligent leader and Malinche as a beautiful and wise woman. Her role in the conquest of Mexico is very well portrayed. Unfortunately, the author emphasizes the cruelty and human sacrifices practiced by the Aztecs throughout the book; although she also mentions some of the beauty of the New World, it is not as fully described as the human sacrifices, which are mentioned nine times. She insists that the natives were savages and ignorant, and adds, "... nor were these people indolent like the Mayans ..." (p. 35). (The Mayans indolent? Who then was responsible for their great civilization?) There is a beautiful description of an Aztec marketplace and baths: "... for the Aztecs bathed daily, a custom we Spaniards frowned upon as dangerous to health" (p. 118).

Nacar, the White Deer, by Treviño, is the story of a white deer and his mute, Mexican shepherd boy, who protected the deer and made it possible for the deer to be presented to the King of Spain in 1630. The Catholic religion in 17th-century Mexico and Spain is very realistically por-

trayed, as is the great poverty and wealth of Mexico City.
And even though "tortillas" are repeatedly mentioned as part
of the Mexican peasants' diet, other Mexican delicacies are
also cited: small flat cakes of cheese, turkey "mole," etc.
The Treasure of Topo-el-Bambo, by O'Dell, shows
life in "the poorest village in all Mexico" in the 1700s. The
story includes many of the favorite stereotypes about Mexico
--bandits, tortillas, fiestas, siestas: "There was time for
a small siesta but he fought back the urge to sleep" (p. 38).
And the main characters are two donkeys that worked in a
mine that sent all its silver to the King of Spain. The two
donkeys became the heroes of Topo-el-Bambo when they
brought back many silver bars and "the poorest village in
all of Mexico suddenly became the richest" (p. 48).

Mexican History

The Mexican Story, by McNeer, purports to tell the
whole "Mexican story," but it only shows the subjective view
of an American tourist in Mexico. It has glaring omissions
about pre-Columbian history, although it emphasizes the human sacrifices of the Aztecs (p. 16). Juana Ines' (p. 31)
complete name is never given. And it ends with a patronizing "American señora" who states, as she addresses Mario,
a poor Mexican boy: "Muchas gracias ... and dropped money
in his hand" (p. 92). Because this story includes legends
and simple anecdotes of Mexican history with beautiful illustrations, it could be useful as supplementary reading in Mexican history.

Mexico

There are several books that give an overview of the

history or the people of Mexico. The following three books
are highly recommended, as they are written by three authors
who seem to know Mexico very well:

Getting to Know Mexico, by Gómez, is a valuable
overall introduction to Mexico with simple descriptions of
life in Mexico. It includes realistic illustrations of a middle
class girl at a Mexican home (p. 15); appetizing descriptions
of the variety of foods and eating habits in Mexico (pp. 19,
20, and 21); the truth about siestas: "There is an old-
fashioned idea that Mexicans take naps or 'siestas' after
lunch. After such a big meal, you could understand why they
might like to. But actually they are far too busy these days
to take siestas except in the regions where it gets very hot
in the afternoon" (p. 20); bargaining in the market (pp. 29,
30, and 31); Independence Day (p. 49); Day of the Dead (p.
50); and Posadas (pp. 54, 55, 56, and 57).

Mexico, by Ross, is an authentic account of various
aspects of Mexico, emphasizing the contrasts in the country
by an author who understands the people and the problems
of Mexico. Unfortunately, some of the photographs are out-
dated. The following chapters are of special interest: Chapter 5, "The Mexican People," for a good description of
"Mestizos" and Indians (p. 35), a historical overview of the
Independence, and "Mexico's greatest president was a wise
and good Indian named Benito Juárez" (p. 45); Chapter 9,
"Industry in Mexico"; Chapter 14, "Mexican Food," which
describes, with superior black and white photographs, tortillas, tamales, tacos, enchiladas, beans, mole, guacamole,
the great variety of tropical fruits, chocolate, etc. It truth-
fully states: "If you should visit Mexico, you would find
that most people living in the cities eat the same kinds of
food you do" (p. 106). Chapter 16, "Handicrafts," has at-

tractive black and white photographs which show the great
variety of Mexican crafts; and Chapter 18, "Mexico's Fiestas,"
has outstanding descriptions of the Independence Day Celebra-
tion (p. 130), religious feast days (p. 131), All Saints Day
and All Souls Day, which are combined with the ancient Indian Day of the Dead, when "The ancient Indians believed
that the dead returned once a year to be fed" (p. 132).   And,
"It is a happy time to welcome the souls of the dead, who
came back to visit their homes on earth" (p. 133).

Here Is Mexico, by Treviño, presents optimistic and
personal "impressions which mean Mexico and which illum-
inate one or another of the qualities of this country and its
people."   She discusses many isolated facts and customs:
pre-Columbian history, the Colonial period, the Revolution,
mountains, rivers and lakes, wealth and poverty, food, arts
and fiestas.   She explains popular misconceptions about Mexico to American readers, such as the common tourists' in-
testinal disorders (p. 180), and highlights positive aspects of
Mexico: "... it is remarkable that there is little if any race
prejudice in Mexico.   Perhaps the subtle and distinguished
Indian civilizations that the Spanish encountered are partly
the explanation for this.   Today in Mexico race prejudice is
almost nonexistent, although it is true that there exists a
certain amount of snobbish prejudice based on economic
status" (p. 74).

Let's Visit Mexico, by Caldwell, is an unfortunate introduction to Mexico as it reinforces several negative impressions.   For example, the book begins by writing about
the Alamo: "From February 23rd until March 6th 1836, a
band of one hundred and eighty-four Texans was besieged by
one thousand Mexicans at a little place called the Alamo.
Every one of the Texans was killed.   There were famous

American names among the dead: Davy Crockett's was one"
(p. 9). There are also several incorrect facts or misinter-
pretations: "For the most part, Indian life in pre-Columbian
times was simple. Many tribes were nomadic ..." (p. 21).
(The author forgot to read about the Mayan, Aztec, Teotihuacan and other cultures.) "During the siesta time, it is
difficult to buy anything in a Mexican town" (p. 74). (The
author has not been in many Mexican towns, because this is
not true.) "With so many holidays, fiestas, and feasts to be
celebrated, Mexican boys and girls have more days off from
school than do American children" (p. 79). (Wrong again!
Mexican children have shorter summer holidays; therefore
they have more three-day weekends than American children
have; but they go to school approximately the same number
of days.) This is a patronizing book written by an author
who neglected to do his homework.

Mexico for Kids, by Swiger, tells children about
Mexico by describing the Pyramids of Teotihuacan, Chapul-
tepec Park, a bullfight, Mexican kids, Taxco, Mexican roads,
agriculture in Mexico and Mexico City. Mistakenly, it describes Maximilian as a "Frenchman" (p. 26). The illustrations show too many barefoot peasants and the book emphasizes the poverty of Mexican children. "Pallaçio de Bellas
Artes" [sic] is misspelled.

Tacho Boy of Mexico, by Darbois, describes the life
of an extremely indigent Mexican boy, who lives in a small
village. His house "has one room with a dirt floor and no
windows or chimney" (p. 14). Black and white photographs
show Tacho's house made with maguey leaves, his sister
making tortillas sitting down on the dirt floor, "serapes,"
"sombreros," and, to complete its "authenticity": "It is the
custom in Mexico to take a nap in the afternoon when the

sun is quite hot. The nap is called a siesta" (p. 22).

Mexican-Americans

The following books present the history and problems of the Mexican-Americans:

The Story of the Mexican Americans, by Acuña, is an excellent introduction to the history of the Mexican-American in the Southwest. It describes the early settlers, life in the old southwest, transportation, trade, laws and government, and the Mexican-American heritage, emphasizing its importance for contemporary life in the southwest. It has superior pictures, drawings and maps.

The Mexican American, by Martinez and Edwards, presents a very readable history of the Mexican-American which emphasizes major developments and explains many aspects of his rich and varied culture. It includes pre-Columbian Mexico, the Age of Exploration, Life in the Spanish Colonies, the Mission Period in California, Mexico's Independence, Reform and Revolution, and Mexican-Americans becoming second-class citizens. It also explains basic historical differences: "The emphasis on obedience to the Spanish Crown and respect for the powerful Catholic Church made it almost impossible for the people to make achievements on their own. The Anglo pioneers, on the other hand, were a rugged and resourceful people with a heritage of freedom and independence. They did not hesitate to fight for what they wanted" (pp. 150-151).

South by Southwest, by Tebbel and Ruiz, highlights Mexican-American achievements, their reasons for immigration, and discrimination against them. It describes the fusion of the pre-Columbian and Spanish world during the

Colonial period in art and architecture (pp. 34-35). It mentions Mexican artists and authors and is perhaps overly optimistic about modern Mexico. Nevertheless, it states: "the
basic cause of Mexico's troubles remains: 'living standards
are low ... a few people have a great deal of money and
most of the others have little'" (p. 89). "Illiteracy is a
major problem" (p. 91). And it discusses corruption of
government employees who "have become corrupt in the taking of bribes" (p. 91). The authors also discuss the many
reasons that are given by Americans and Mexicans for the
Mexican-American War (p. 96).

Small Hands, Big Hands, by Weiner, describes the
working and living conditions of seven migrant workers and
their families. Unfortunately, the author emphasizes only
negative aspects of Mexico and materialistic benefits of life
in the U.S.: "I like it better in the United States.... He
makes better money here" (p. 3). "Over in Mexico there
isn't a single car, just cheap buses that carry people around"
(p. 5). "In Mexico ... if they see you have a television or
a 21-jewel wrist watch they'll try to steal it when you're not
home. That's why people have guns over there" (p. 11).
"The dogs in Mexico have rabies with saliva running out of
their mouths" (p. 11). "He only loses his temper when he
drinks too much" (p. 23).

Graciela--A Mexican-American Child Tells Her Story,
by Molnar, stresses the economic hardships of a twelve-
year-old girl and her family who go to Michigan to work in
the fields, picking fruits and vegetables. It describes their
living conditions: "If you want hot water you have to heat it
up and the stove it only has two burners and no oven. And
you have to go outside to a well to get the water with a
pump" [sic] (unnumbered). It mentions prejudice and their

"pride" in being Chicano: "Another time a teacher in the
high school called my brother Eleazar a wetback, and he
doesn't like to be called that. He says he's a Chicano, a
Mexican-American who's proud of it" (unnumbered). Pride
is a marvelous thing ... but how can this book help Mexican-
American children feel any dignity about their own identity?

EVALUATION AND FOLLOW-UP ACTIVITIES

1. Ask the students to describe at least one reason for Span-
    ish Colonial Expansion. The description should include
    the desire for wealth, gold, and precious stones, and the
    acquisition of new territory.

2. Ask the students to describe at least one outstanding
    characteristic of the following cultures: Mayan, Teoti-
    huacan, Toltec, Mixtec-Zapotec, and Aztec. Students
    may also be asked to draw a picture representing their
    favorite pre-Columbian design, pyramid, sculpture, etc.

3. Ask the students to identify at least one characteristic
    in architecture, lifestyle, or customs of Colonial Mexico
    which illustrates the fusion of the Spanish with pre-Colum-
    bian cultures. Important examples of the fusion of the
    two cultures are seen in:

        architecture, art, and folklore

        lifestyle: (Mestizo: intermarriage between Indian and
            Spanish)

        customs: food, fiestas, religion

4. Ask the students to describe:

    a. The political situation in Mexico and the U.S. prior
        to the Mexican-American War. The description
        might include at least one of the following:

        (1) The poverty of Mexico

        (2) The power of the Catholic Church in Mexico

      (3) The annexation of Texas and the slavery question

   b. The upheaval that occurred during the War. The description might include:

      (1) The cunning of Santa Ana and his deals with Polk

      (2) The War's unpopularity in the U.S.

   c. The major results of the War.

      (1) Loss of 50% of the Mexican territory to the U.S.

      (2) The American Civil War

5. Mexican-Americans today:

   a. Ask the students to describe at least one economic or social problem of Mexico today. The description should include at least one of the following:

      (1) Extreme wealth vs. extreme poverty

      (2) High unemployment

      (3) High illiteracy rate

   b. Ask the students to describe why poverty is the main reason for immigration to the U.S. Students might state that many Mexicans come to the U.S. to search for work and a better life.

   c. Ask the students to describe at least one result of this immigration. The results of this immigration should include at least one of the following:

      (1) barrios

      (2) illiteracy

      (3) unskilled labor

      (4) migrant and field workers

      (5) ethnic isolation.

<u>Grades: Seventh-High School</u>

OUTCOMES

1. Identify Spanish achievements in literature and art and
   important customs of Spain in the 16th century. Describe reasons for Spanish colonial expansion.

2. Pre-Columbian Mexico: describe the achievements of
   Mayan, Teotihuacan, Toltec, Mixtec-Zapotec, and Aztec
   cultures.

3. Colonial Mexico--fusion of two cultures: identify characteristics of architecture, lifestyle, and customs which
   illustrate the fusion of the Spanish with the pre-Columbian cultures.

4. Mexican-American conflict: describe the political situation in Mexico and the U.S. prior to the War, the upheavals that occurred during the War, and the major results of the War.

5. Mexican-Americans today:

   a. Describe the economic and social problems of Mexi-
      co today.

   b. Describe why poverty is the main reason for immi-
      gration to the U.S.

   c. Describe the results of immigration.

BOOKS*

*Acuña, Rudy. A Mexican American Chronicle. American
   Book, 1971.

---

*Only books marked with an asterisk are recommended titles.

*Bruckner, Karl. Viva Mexico. Burke Publishing Co.,
    1960.

*Coy, Harold. Chicano Roots Go Deep. Dodd, Mead and
    Company, 1975.

*Coy, Harold. The Mexicans. Little Brown and Company,
    1970.

De Garza, Patricia. Chicanos--the Story of Mexican Amer-
    icans. Messner, 1973.

*Gallenkamp, Charles. Maya: The Riddle and Rediscovery
    of a Lost Civilization. David McKay, 1976.

Garcia, Joe Dell and Mabel Otis Robison. Come Along to
    Mexico. Denison, 1965.

González, Rodolfo. I Am Joaquín. Bantam, 1967.

Martinez, Elizabeth Sutherland and Enriqueta Longeaux y
    Vasquez. Viva la Raza!: the Struggle of the Mexican-
    American People. Doubleday, 1974.

*Meier, Matt S. and Feliciano Rivera, editors. Readings
    on La Raza: The Twentieth Century. Hill and Wang,
    1974.

*Meltzer, Milton. Bound for the Rio Grande: the Mexican
    Struggle, 1845-1850. Knopf, 1974.

*Nava, Julian. Mexican Americans Past, Present, and Fu-
    ture. American Book Company, 1969.

Ortego, Philip D., editor. We Are Chicanos: An Anthology
    of Mexican-American Literature. Washington Square
    Press, 1973.

Pinchot, Jane. The Mexicans in America. Lerner Publica-
    tions, 1973.

*Polland, Madeleine. Alhambra. Doubleday, 1970.

Polley, Judith. Val Verde. Delacorte Press, 1974.

Prago, Albert. Strangers in Their Own Land. Four Winds
    Press, 1973.

*Traven, B. The Cotton-Pickers. Hill and Wang, 1969.

DISCUSSION

Mexican-American students should be proud of the
great heritage that is legitimately theirs. Through an understanding of the marvelous richness of pre-Columbian, Spanish, Mexican, and Mexican-American cultures, students may
develop the genuine self-respect that only comes from a true
knowledge of one's own history and background. The different historical periods of Spain, Mexico and the Southwest
may be further studied through additional books. The following books attempt to offer an overall introduction to the historical greatness of Spain, Mexico and the Southwest. These
books are discussed in a chronological historical order:

Pre-Columbian Mexico

Maya: The Riddle and Rediscovery of a Lost Civilization, by Gallenkamp, is a very readable and well-documented
history of the Mayans--their obscure origins, their remarkable
artistic and intellectual achievements, their social structure,
and their mysterious decline. It is a vivid reconstruction of
the art, literature, science, and ritualism embodied in Mayan culture, with a description of the work of important
archaeologists and their discoveries. The greatness of the
Mayans of the Classic Period is effectively described by the
author: "Such pursuits as mathematics, hieroglyphic writing,
astronomy, and calendrics opened limitless new scientific
and philosophical vistas. Stone sculpture gave permanent
expression to aesthetic concepts previously impossible to ex-
ecute ..." (p. 69). And, "Another notable feature of Maya

mathematics was the principle of the zero.... Even the
Greeks and Romans had no knowledge of the zero ..." (p.
76).

Spain

Alhambra, by Polland, is an engrossing historical
novel in which a brother and sister survive a Moorish attack
and grow up in the Palace of the Alhambra in Granada.   It
has interesting descriptions of the life and customs of Spain
in the years 1481 to 1492, emphasizing the beauty of the
Palace--its fountains, courtyards and trees; the beginning of
the reign of King Ferdinand and Queen Isabella, and the pride
of the Spanish people.   There is a gentle love story involving Juanito, a Spaniard, and Nahid, who is presented as a
Moorish princess.

Mexico

The Mexicans, by Coy, is an outstanding history of
Mexico which includes a brief introduction to Mexico and
how it is different from the U.S., the Olmec and Aztec cultures, the Spanish Conquest (with both the Spanish and Indian versions), Colonial Mexico, the Independence, the Mexican-American War, the Reform movement, Porfirio Díaz
and industrialization, the Revolution and modern Mexico.
The only weak part in this book is perhaps the chapter on
modern Mexico, because it ignores many unpleasant economic
facts of Mexico today.   Unfortunately, it is not true that:
"Though our population has multiplied, we no longer import
food as in Porfirian times.   Instead, we export it" (p. 285).
It does not mention unemployment, the tremendous birth rate,
or illiteracy; instead, it states: "Higher education, formerly

limited to a few thousand youths, is the privilege of hundreds of thousands" (p. 289). But this is a spirited history book, as when it states: "Santa Ana's conscience was flexible" (p. 197).

Come Along to Mexico, by Garcia and Robison, is a cursory introduction to Mexico. Although it includes the Conquest, colonization, archaeological ruins, places and people, education, habits and customs, and developments in Mexico, the authors generalize instead of explaining, as when they describe a pre-Columbian design: "The conquerors saw strange carvings which they could not understand" (p. 15). It erroneously states: "Pueblo of Tenochtitlan" (p. 16). (Tenochtitlan was a city, by either pre-Columbian or modern standards.) And, it states about a "cargadore" [sic]: "... he can live on tortillas which he takes with him" (pp. 108 and 109). The following words in Spanish are misspelled:

"Moreles" [sic] (p. 37)   "Moralos" [sic] (p. 101)
"Tloquepoque" [sic] (p. 102) "huarachas" [sic] (p. 108)

Foreign Intervention in Mexico

Val Verde, by Polley, is a historical novel which describes Antoinette Dubec's feelings toward a Mexican officer, Ramon Chavez, during the years of Maximilian's and Carlota's reign in war-torn Mexico. It describes Antoinette's thoughts as a young woman; her sorrow as she learns of her father's death; and her love and courtship with her handsome officer. It superficially mentions the conflicts between the Juaristas and the Loyalists, but it does not explain Mexico's political or economic conditions at the time.

Mexican-American War

Bound for the Rio Grande: The Mexican Struggle
1845-1850, by Meltzer, is an excellent historical account of
the Mexican-American War. It presents, through letters,
diaries and writings of Mexican and American people who
lived at the time, both sides of the struggle: the poverty of
Mexico; the power of the Catholic Church in Mexico; the
problem of the annexation of Texas and the slavery question;
Mexico's politicians ("'Of all the sly schemers in the history
of Mexico,' says Professor Ramon E. Ruiz, 'Santa Ana was
the master'" (p. 97)); it quotes Justo Sierra on Santa Ana's
cunningness and Santa Ana's deals with Polk; and it explains
why the Mexican War has been neglected: "... lies rooted
in the guilt that we as a nation have come to feel about it
... who denounced the war as a cynical land-grab from a
neighbor too weak to defend herself' (p. 262).

Mexican Revolution

Viva Mexico, by Bruckner, is a fascinating historical
novel of the Mexican Revolution of 1910. Juanito, an Indian
boy, frees Miguel, the hero and a courageous man who
wanted to help the oppressed Mexican peasants. It describes
the dismal conditions in the haciendas before the Revolution:
the eighteen-hour work day, child-labor, the "tiendas de
raya," and the inheritance of debts. About Díaz' government, it states: "Porfirio Díaz has reduced Mexico to a
slave state. People abroad speak of our country with con-
tempt for its corrupt bureaucracy and the greed of its land-
owners who suck the blood of the workers like leeches ..."
(p. 188).

The Cotton-Pickers, by Traven, is an engaging histor-

ical novel of Revolutionary Mexico in 1915. Gales, the main
character, picks cotton, works in a bakery and drives a
thousand head of cattle more than 350 miles to earn enough
money to buy a shirt, or a pair of shoes, or a woman, or
a glass of tequila. It describes the pathetic conditions of
life in Mexico at the time: "I always told you we shouldn't
have come here. This country is stark, raving mad.
There's no law and order here. You can go on paying your
taxes, and paying them on the dot, but you never get a say
in anything" (p. 105).

Mexican-Americans

Mexican Americans Past, Present, and Future, by
Nava, is an outstandingly honest and well-documented history
of the Mexican-Americans, written in a simple and precise
manner. It explains the history, achievements and problems
of Spain as they relate to the history of Mexico and the Southwest; Mexico from its pre-Columbian greatness to its economic problems and reasons for Mexican migration to the
U.S.; the history of the Mexican-Americans in Texas, New
Mexico, Arizona and California; and Mexican-Americans to-
day--their achievements, goals, and conflicts. It also has
excellent black and white photographs that contribute im-
mensely to the interesting text.

A Mexican American Chronicle, by Acuña, is an in-
depth study of the history and the identity crisis of Mexicans
in the U.S. It includes excellent photographs and well-documented information about pre-Columbian history and cultural
achievements; the Spanish historical, artistic, and literary
background; the economic problems of Mexican-Americans;
and it mentions many positive aspects about Mexico, such as:

"While in many countries military men or sports figures are
national heroes, in Mexico the intellectual is the true hero
and is revered by the Mexican people" (p. 71). The book
ends with an extensive discussion of Chicano militant leaders,
ideas, controversial topics, and articles.

(See discussion of Chicano Roots Go Deep, by Coy,
under Lifestyle, Grades: Seventh-High School, pp. 65 and 66.)

Readings on La Raza: The Twentieth Century, by
Meier, provides a chronological and topical representation
of Chicano history in the 20th century. It presents important
and controversial events and issues relating to Chicano history and stresses the serious problem of Mexican immigration to the U.S. throughout its six sections. It describes
the "low educational levels and desperate poverty" (p. 81) of
many Mexicans in the 1950s; the repatriation of 300,000 Mexicans (p. 95); the irrational prejudice that the Mexicans encountered in California (p. 115); the concern about the illegal wetbacks (p. 161); and the low wages earned by farmers
in Mexico: "That explains why so many men are anxious to
get seasonal employment on farms in the United States" (p.
169). And, "The wetback is a hungry human being. His
need of food and clothing is immediate and pressing" (p.
192).

We Are Chicanos: An Anthology of Mexican-American
Literature, edited by Ortego, is an angry and passionate attack by several Chicano authors. The tone of the writings,
as exemplified by Armando Rendon's feelings, is: "I owe
my life to my Chicano people. They rescued me from the
Anglo kiss of death, the monolingual, monocultural, and color-
less Gringo society" (p. 87). It includes sections on folklore, feelings, political slogans, poetry, drama, and fiction.
I believe that this book tries to undervalue one culture--the

Anglo culture--to represent the greatness of the Chicano culture. Is this necessary? Why can't we respect and appreciate the admirable traits of both the Mexican-American and
Anglo culture?

I am Joaquín, by González, is a poem with excellent
black and white photographs that describes the history of the
Mexican and Mexican-American people. With text in Spanish
and English it narrates the author's feelings about important
historical incidents and the Chicano movement in America.

Strangers in Their Own Land, by Prago, traces the
history of Mexican-Americans starting with the Conquest of
Mexico and the American Southwest. It describes the War
of 1846, the "gold rush" in California; and the Anglo conquest
of Texas, New Mexico and Arizona. The author tells the
stories of Benito Juárez, Emiliano Zapata, Francisco Villa,
and the recent efforts of César Chávez and other Mexican-
American leaders.

The Mexicans in America, by Pinchot, presents a
brief history of the Mexicans in the United States--their life
in the American Southwest before statehood, the U.S. acqui-
sition of their land, and the individual contributions of Mexicans to American life. Unfortunately, no bibliography is
given.

Chicanos--the Story of Mexican Americans, by De
Garza, explores the causes of Mexican immigration to the
U.S. and discusses the adaptation and contribution of Mexican-Americans to the U.S. Very superficially it explains
the early discriminatory laws that have caused many Mexican-Americans to become bitter and angry. The author
sympathizes with the militant position of some groups: "To
change these conditions, Chicano student groups have used
actions as well as words. They have declared a need for

more militant 'revolutionary activity,' and so have held political rallies, marched in picket lines, published Chicano
school newspapers, and staged school walk-outs." Although
it claims to be strictly historical, it does not include a bibliography.

Viva la Raza!: the Struggle of the Mexican-American
People, by Martinez and Vasquez, is an emotional, rambling,
and repetitive condemnation of Anglo society which ignores
many historical assertions. It is written in an angry and
bitter style: "Our people are on the march in all levels of
life, awakening and demanding justice.... After decades of
being lynched and displaced ..." (p. 2). "... and refuse to
be divided any longer as the white man has tried to keep us
divided for centuries" (p. 3). "... it is in our Chicanismo
that we have come to see all of the cancer in the dominant
white society ..." (p. 6). "... and throw off the BIG LIES
of the Anglo society and its institutions" (p. 9). It mis-
represents pre-Columbian history, as when it states that the
Aztecs had an equalitarian society: "Some of them did have
finer clothes or a bigger variety of food than others, but on
the whole everyone prospered or suffered together ..." (p.
15). It does not mention the abuses of Mexican politicians
and leaders toward their own people when describing the
Mexican-American War and General Santa Ana (p. 62). Regrettably this book portrays Anglo society as "all black" and
Chicano society as "all white." I believe that this book is
an indolent indictment of a whole culture--the Anglo culture--
and that it insults the intelligence of any thinking or educated
reader.

EVALUATION AND FOLLOW-UP ACTIVITIES

1. Ask the students to identify at least two of the following:

    Cervantes   The Inquisition
    Velasquez   Phillip II
    The Catholic Church

    Ask the students to describe at least one reason for
    Spanish Colonial expansion. The description should in-
    clude the desire for wealth, gold and precious stones,
    and the acquisition of new territory.

2. Ask the students to describe at least one outstanding
    characteristic of the following cultures: Mayan, Teoti-
    huacan, Toltec, Mixtec-Zapotec, and Aztec. Students
    may also be asked to draw a picture representing their
    favorite pre-Columbian design, pyramid, sculpture, etc.

3. Ask the students to identify at least one characteristic
    in architecture, lifestyle, or customs of Colonial Mexico
    which illustrate the fusion of the Spanish with pre-Colum-
    bian cultures. Important examples of the fusion of the
    two cultures are seen in:

    architecture, art, and folklore

    lifestyle: (Mestizo: Intermarriage between Indian
        and Spanish)

    customs: food, fiestas, religion

4. Ask the students to describe:

    a. The political situation in Mexico and the U.S. prior
        to the Mexican-American War. The description
        might include at least one of the following:

        (1) The poverty of Mexico

        (2) The power of the Catholic Church in Mexico

        (3) The annexation of Texas and the slavery ques-
             tion

    b. The upheaval that occurred during the War. The
        description might include:

        (1)   The cunning of Santa Ana and his deals with Polk

        (2)   The War's unpopularity in the U.S.

    c. The major results of the War:

        (1)   Loss of 50% of the Mexican territory to the U.S.

        (2)   The American Civil War

5.   Mexican-Americans today:

    a. Ask the students to describe at least one economic or social problem of Mexico today. The description should include at least one of the following:

        (1) Extreme wealth vs. extreme poverty

        (2) High unemployment

        (3) High illiteracy rate

    b. Ask the students to describe why poverty is the main reason for immigration to the U.S. Students might state that many Mexicans come to the U.S. to search for work and a better life.

    c. Ask the students to describe at least one result of this immigration. The results of this immigration should include at least one of the following:

        (1) barrios

        (2) illiteracy

        (3) unskilled labor

        (4) migrant and field workers

        (5) ethnic isolation.

APPENDICES

In my discussions with many teachers, librarians, or parents, about books about Mexican and Mexican-American children and adolescents, someone invariably asks about "bilingual books." Because the term "bilingual" has come to mean different things to different people, I have learned to ask for clarification of the term before I express my own opinion of such books as: bilingual books, books written in Spanish by Spanish-speaking authors, Spanish translations of books by American authors, books that describe bilingual people, or Spanish grammar books. Also misleading is that section of libraries which is often called "Bilingual," where a collection of the forementioned books is found.

Because of the constantly increasing number of Spanish-speaking people in the U.S., it is indeed essential to consider the literature for children and young adults of Spanish-speaking countries. The following articles express my concerns and are the result of several years of investigating the literature for young readers in Spanish from Mexico and Spain. "The Dilemma of Selecting Spanish-Language Books" introduces the reader to common practices and popular misconceptions in selecting Spanish-language books in the United States. "A Sad Truth: The State of the Literature for Children and Adolescents of Mexico" describes the unfortunate scarcity of books for young readers in Mexico. And "A Heartfelt Plea: Notes on Books for Children and Adolescents

from Spain'' exposes the interested reader to the unexplored
wealth of books from Spain.

APPENDIX A

THE DILEMMA OF SELECTING
SPANISH-LANGUAGE BOOKS*

As I examined the Spanish-language children's books
at the 1976 Combined Book Exhibit, recommended by the
Children's Services Division's (CSD) Selection of Foreign
Children's Books Committee, I was reminded of the careless
and thoughtless manner in which many teachers and librarians
purchase books in Spanish for children and young adults.
This exhibit was a perfect example of what is definitely
wrong with many collections of books in Spanish for children
and young adults in public and school libraries in the United
States. The CSD selectors chose mainly Spanish translations
of American and German scientific, technical, and historical
books. And, in their fiction section, which consists of only
five books, they included translations of books by Alfred
Hitchcock, Jules Verne, Lewis Wallace, and Ralph Hermanns.
This to me is not selection, but a random choice of books
translated into Spanish without regard for children's interests,
reading abilities, or cultural identities.

I constantly hear the same complaints from librarians
who occasionally purchase books in Spanish: "The bindings
are bad." "The books fall apart." "The margins, the paper,

*Reprinted by permission from School Library Journal 23:92
(October 1976), published by R. R. Bowker Company/A Xer-
ox Corporation.

the illustrations, and the size of the print are inadequate."
"There are many differences in the Spanish language spoken
in the U.S.--our students don't understand Castilian." "I
have problems with the distributors and I can not purchase
books abroad." "We buy them, but they are not used," etc.
I know that many of these complaints are partly true and
there are critical problems in selecting books in Spanish for
children and young adults. I sympathize with librarians who
are truly concerned about the quality of their collections, but
I think it is time that we seriously consider our goals in selecting books in Spanish for readers. The basic purposes of
offering books in Spanish should be considered by anyone es-
tablishing such a collection for children and young adults.

Bicultural or Bilingual?

I have always supported the contention that a bicultural emphasis is more important than a bilingual one. De-
spite the fact that one is indeed fortunate to be able to speak,
read, and write in two languages, and that language is a
marvelous skill to have in order to appreciate and understand
another culture, language learning should not be an end in
itself. Many library collections for children in Spanish seem
to be selected without regard for the cultural greatness of
the Spanish-speaking peoples.

Just as any Anglo child grows up appreciating the language of Shakespeare, so should Spanish-speaking children
grow up appreciating the language of Cervantes. Spanish-
speaking children should be exposed to the writings, feelings,
and thoughts of Spanish-speaking authors. They should become aware of the greatness of their cultural heritage. And,
as no one book will satisfy the reading interests of all chil-

dren, we should offer a diversity of books in Spanish that
may satisfy the curiosity and excite the attention of many
children.

Librarians who select books in Spanish should consider the writings of Spanish-speaking authors who are inti-
mately aware of the sensitivities of their own background;
they should consider the immense selection of Spanish, Mexican, and South American folk tales and legends; and they
should consider art books, history books, classical adaptations, historical fiction, and poetry books which are available
in Spanish and which explore the culture of Spanish-speaking
people.

Regional Distinctions

Just as any Anglo child can read a children's book
published in England, so can any Spanish-speaking child read
any children's book published in Spain, Puerto Rico, or Mexico. There are differences in the Spanish pronunciation of
Spaniards, Cubans, or Mexicans, but they are not as distinct
as the difference in English pronunciation between American
and British people. The differences in the Spanish language
pronunciations among South American, Mexican, and Spanish
people can be better illustrated as comparable with the re-
gional English language pronunciation differences of North
American people: southerners, northerners, California natives, midwesterners, etc. I have never heard any librarian
say that a child who lives in California cannot read a book
published in New York.

The Castilian Myth

The statement, "Chicano children do not understand

Castilian," only means that many Chicano, Puerto Rican,
and other Spanish-speaking children in the U.S. grow up cul-
turally deprived, and thus do not speak Spanish or appreciate
their own culture.   Language is only one aspect of one's cultural identity and Spanish-speaking children should be offered
the opportunity to select attractive books written in Spanish
regardless of where they are published.

Quality

Unfortunately, books published abroad in Spanish do
not have the excellent reinforced bindings that librarians un-
derstandably expect.   But the attractive illustrations, wide
margins, and high quality of paper and print of many of the
books published in Spanish make rebinding a worthwhile al-
ternative.   Also, the average cost of books for children published abroad is considerably less than the average cost of
books published in the U.S., thereby making rebinding a
valuable investment.

Translations

Because "bilingual stories" are now fashionable in
many communities, librarians should be cautioned against
purchasing only Spanish translations of popular North American authors, such as Richard Scarry, Lois Lenski, and others.   Translations and "bilingual stories" may be used to
supplement a collection and to offer a much needed variety,
but they should never take the place of genuine books that
reaffirm a child's identity and enrich his or her life as an
individual human being.

I do not believe in checklists or guidelines for books
in Spanish because I cannot explain literary or artistic ex-

cellence.   I cannot describe what factors develop insights
into a child's life.   I do not know in what sequence we can
interest a child in reading as a lifelong activity.   But as a
mother, librarian, and educator, I can only assume that a
wide variety of books in Spanish, selected by genuinely concerned librarians, will entice Spanish-speaking young people
to explore the marvelous world of books in our libraries.

APPENDIX B

A SAD TRUTH: THE STATE OF THE LITERATURE FOR CHILDREN AND ADOLESCENTS OF MEXICO*

Mexican children and adolescents should have literature available to enrich their lives as individual human beings,
to develop insights and understandings into their own lives
and the realities of Mexico, to become aware of the greatness
of their cultural heritage, and to develop an interest in reading as a leisure-time activity. But, unfortunately, there has
not been a serious or dedicated effort in Mexico to collect or
disseminate its literature for young readers.

The history of Mexico has left a fascinating legacy of
cultural background to its people. The pre-Columbian period
has bequeathed important vestiges of several splendid and
significant cultures: Teotihuacán with its majestic pyramids
and temples; Chichen-Itzá, Uxmal and Palenque as witnesses
of the enlightened Mayans; the warriors at Tula guarding the
remains of the Toltecs; and the monumental sculptures of the
Aztecs that testify to their scientific and technological knowledge.

The Conquest period united the Spanish and the Indian
race, giving to the Mexican people both language and religion,

---

*This article was taken from a larger work, Mexico and Its
Literature for Children and Adolescents, Special Study #15,
published by the Center for Latin American Studies, Arizona
State University, September, 1977.

124

while enriching their cities with Spanish architectural beauty.
The nineteenth century was a period of political intervention.
The Reform Movement adopted a new Constitution that sepa-
rated the powers of church and state. The twentieth century
began with a powerful oligarchy controlling the financial,
agricultural, and business life of the country. The Revolution of 1910 started as a rebellion against the misery and
ignorance in which most of the people lived.

Modern Mexico has serious economic and educational
problems. Some of the critical educational handicaps are illiteracy; expanding populations of school-age children; rela-
tively few children in school, and these often attending for
very few years; teachers inadequate in number and poorly
trained; schools frozen in traditional patterns unrelated to
modern needs; and unequally distributed educational opportunities. A further hindrance to the educational development of
Mexico is the scarcity of books in Spanish and the neglect
and loss of the pre-Columbian mythology, folklore, and traditions.

Many Mexican educators, such as José Vasconcelos,
Alfredo Ibarra, and Juana Manrique de Lara, have expressed
their concern for the lack of books for children and adolescents. Translations of authors of the last century are most
of the literary selections for young readers available in Spanish in Mexican bookstores. It should also be noted that
Mexican schools do not have libraries and that children's
books may not be checked out from the public libraries.

In 1966 Torres Quintero, a well-known Mexican educator, expressed his unhappiness about the use of books in
Mexican schools. He wrote:

> ... I know that the books used in schools, and
> how they are used do not construct, but destroy

... yes, I curse them because they are misused
(Torres Quintero, p. 88).

Many Mexican writers have expressed very traditional
ideas regarding the adequate use of children's literature.
They insist on the importance of using literature to educate
the sensibility of children by helping them to distinguish and
appreciate the valuable and to teach the beauty, the graceful-
ness and the virtue of existence. They also believe that literature must promote feelings that ennoble children and leave
them with useful knowledge. Antonio Robles, who was the
most influential person in children's literature in Mexico for
thirty-three years, advocated correcting and modifying all
traditional fairy tales because fairy tales encouraged murder-
ers or evildoers. The well-known teacher Berta Von Glumer
affirmed that classical fables were not written for children.

Manuel González Flores defended the reading of com-
ics, explaining that they contribute to the literacy campaign
in the country. Herminio Almendros objected to the fantasy
and the misrepresentation of life and reality that are evident
in Western books written for children.

Authors of the Nineteenth Century

There are a few authors who wrote or collected
stories for children and adolescents in the nineteenth century. In 1816 José Joaquín Fernández Lizardi wrote El
periquillo sarniento (The itching parrot) which is frequently
referred to as the first Latin American novel. It is a long,
moralistic, educational novel which examined the vices and
virtues of Mexican society.

Ignacio M. Altamirano's novel, La navidad en las
montañas (Christmas in the mountains), is required reading

for all secondary students in Mexico. It is a religious novel
which describes Christmas celebrations in a Mexican town.

Manuel Gutiérrez Nájera wrote moralistic short stories
which describe the sad conditions of life of many Mexicans.
José Rosas Moreno was the first Mexican author to write exclusively for children. Unfortunately his cheerful and amusing fables are not read by Mexican children today. And
Juan de Dios Peza was the first Mexican author to write
poetry for children. His educational and moralistic poems
were intended to teach young people to be "good."

Authors of the Twentieth Century

There are several Mexican authors who have written
or are writing books during the twentieth century. Very
often these authors write literature for adults, but one or
more of their books are read by adolescents. Such is the
case with Ermilo Abreu Gómez's novel, Canek, which describes the poverty and abuse of the Mayan Indians of Yucatan; and Celedonio Serrano Martínez's novel, El cazador y
sus perros (The hunter and his dogs), which describes the
author's feelings for the Mexican countryside.

Santos Caballero's Las aventuras de Pipiolo (Pipiolo's
adventures), Arturo Gutiérrez Arias' El mensaje de Fobos
(The message from Fobos), Flavio Gutiérrez Zacarias' Shunco, Irene G. de Lanz's Tismiche, and Blanca de Stefano's
Noriki are novels that were written for adolescents.

A few authors have written short stories for adolescents. Angel de Campo described in his short stories the
daily life of Mexican people of extreme poverty. José Juan
Tablada described Mexico, and Amado Nervo described his
childhood in an amusing story.

The most active group now writing short stories for
adolescents in Mexico is the Grupo Ocelotl. This group of
young Mexican authors has published several collections of
short stories that describe the life and problems of today's
Mexican adolescents.

Some authors have had published only one story for
children. Juan Campuzano's Jesusón, Alfredo Peña Cardona's
La máscara que hablaba (The mask that talked) and Irene G.
de Lanz's El parguito rosado (Little pink snapper) are outstanding stories with beautiful illustrations for children.

Francisco Gabilondo Soler has written many delightful
nursery rhymes about talking animals for young children.
Indiana Nájera and Josefina Zendejas wrote moralistic and
educational stories. Berta Von Glumer's and Luz María Serradell's stories about nature and things common to children
are very well known by kindergarten teachers.

Blanca Lydia Trejo has been one of the most active
authors of literature for children in Mexico. Her stories,
exquisitely illustrated in color, always end with an emphatic
moral. She has adapted for children well-known Mexican
legends, adding her own moral to each legend.

Antonio Robles is one of the most controversial of the
writers who have published in Mexico. The Ministry of Education has published and praised all his books of stories for
children. Recently a few educators have openly criticized
his style and his characters. His stories are regarded by
many teachers and educators as difficult to understand because of long, dull narrations and descriptions.

The beautiful legends of Mexico have been collected
by Pablo González Casanova in Cuentos indígenas (Indigenous
stories) and Alfredo Ibarra in Cuentos y leyendas de México
(Stories and legends of Mexico). Unfortunately, they are not

A Bicultural Heritag

Aurea. Bibliotecas infantiles. México:
Nacional de Bibliotecarios y Archivistas, 196

. "El cuento en México." Revista hispánica
3 (1942), 25-31.

n, Moisés. "Cómo fomentar el hábito de la
Gaceta pedagógica, Noviembre 1971.

o, Wigberto, y A. García Ruiz. Historia de
México: Instituto Nacional de Antropología e
1962.

anrique de. "Literatura infantil y juvenil."
y el pueblo, Marzo-Abril 1957.

teratura mexicana para niños." Boletín bib-
de la Escuela Nacional de Bibliotecarios y
as, Enero y Febrero 1957.

aría Luisa Cresta de. "De la literatura in-
Cuadernos americanos, Enero-Febrero 1954.

literatura infantil o 50 respuestas de Antonio
México: Ediciones Ateneo, 1966.

antil." Forjadores, Noviembre-Diciembre

del Carmen. Cuentos americanos. México:
a de Educación Pública, 1946.

uatl." Forjadores, Abril 1972.

era, Joaquín. "Ignacio Altamirano un refor-
tegro." Forjadores, Mayo 1972.

"Apuntes de actualidad." El nacional, En-
947.

e Estados Americanos. Informe del grupo de
obre libros para niños. México: O.E.A.,

a. "El cuento, la fábula y el niño." El
l pueblo, Mayo-Junio 1956.

available to Mexican children or adolescents.   Only adult,
scholarly editions have been published.

Amado Nervo is a very well-known Mexican poet and
some of his brief and candid poems are enjoyed by Mexican
children.   José Juan Tablada wrote simple poems around
Mexican themes.   Luz María Serradell has written simple
and delightful rhymes and riddles for young children.

The only book of literature for children and adolescents published between the years 1970 and 1976 by the Ministry of Education is a reprint of the 1924 edition of Bernardo
J. Gastelum's anthology, Lecturas clásicas para niños (Classical readings for children).   It contains selections of the
world's classical literature condensed for children and adolescents.   Secondary students are still expected to read
Amado Nervo's 1933 anthology, Lecturas literarias (Literary
readings), which includes selections of Mexican, Latin American, and Spanish classics.

Vicente T. Mendoza's outstanding collection of Mexican
lyrics, from lullabies to singing games, is a one-of-a-kind
collection of the abundant Mexican musical folklore.

The Future?

The future of the literature for children and adolescents in Mexico does not appear to be too encouraging.   Many
educators, librarians, and teachers regret the lack of literature available.   Mrs. Irene G. de Lanz, a well-known Mexican writer, expressed her sad experiences in writing for
children and stated her belief that the Ministry of Education
is not interested in encouraging literature for children and
adolescents.   Mr. Miguel Palacios, subdirector of the Library "Mexico," thinks that there are not enough incentives

A Bicultural Heritage

for authors to write for children. Teachers, professors, people connected with bookstores, and educators at the Ministry of Education agree that authors receive very little support in Mexico and that traditionally Mexico has not been interested in any educational materials for children or adolescents.

There is much to be done in every field of education in Mexico today. The country has serious economic and social problems that it is trying to solve at the same time that it endeavors to meet the ever-increasing demand for education of all its citizens. The Ministry of Education is training teachers, building schools, publishing textbooks and servicing libraries. But this great effort does not fulfill the reading needs of the children and adolescents of Mexico. Much work still needs to be done to offer the beginning of a basic literature for them.

The reality of Mexico's many great and important needs has led to undervaluing or ignoring the provision of literature for children and adolescents as too unrealistic or exorbitant a goal at this stage of its development. The children and adolescents of Mexico have an urgent need for literature written especially for them, taking into account their environment, thoughts, needs, and feelings and the great cultural heritage that is legitimately theirs.

BIBLIOGRAPHY*

Reference Works of Interest to Adults

Abreu Gómez, Ermilo. "Educador, apóstol del idioma."
Forjadores, Enero 1972.

*All journals cited are published in Mexico.

_____. "La ens
pueblo, no. 4

Aguilar Ocejo, Ang
retaría de Ed

Almendros, Hermin
México: Edic

Barlow, Genevieve.
tale." Folklo
ark, Delaware

Bravo Villasante, C
eratura infant

Cardona Peña, Alfr
fantil." El li
43-56.

Carson, W. E. Me
York: Macmil

Departamento de Bil
Pública. Dire
mexicana. Mé
1962.

Díaz Cárdenas, Leó
Primera parte.

Ebel, Robert L. (ed
London: Macm

Flores, Dinorah. B
ico: Impreso
M.A.A., 1952.

Gill, Clark C. Edu
U.S. Governme

Gómez, Aurora M.
Diccionario de
versidad Nacion

González Flores, Ma
eta." El libro
40.

Guzmán Muñoz,
Escuela

Ibarra, Alfredo
moderna,

Jiménez Alarcó
lectura."

Jiménez Moren
México.
Historia,

Lara, Juana M
El libro

_____. "Li
liográfico
Archivist

Leguizamón, M
fantil."

_____. De
Robles.

"Literatura inf
1971.

Millán, María
Secretar

"Mitología Ná

Murrieta Cabr
mador ín

Neck, Mónico.
ero 8, 1

Organización
trabajo
1971.

Palacios, Ade
libro y

Paz Rivera, Helia. "La publicaciones mexicanas para niños." Unpublished paper, México, December 1960.

Pellowski, Anne. The world of children's literature. New York: R. R. Bowker, 1968.

Perez y Contreras, María Esther. La literatura infantil en el jardín de niños. México: Secretaría de Educación Pública, 1970.

R. A. S. "El cuento infantil." El libro y el pueblo, Noviembre 1955.

Robles, Antonio. "Abril en España y en México." El libro y el pueblo, no. 51 (Abril 1969), 21-23.

_____. De literatura infantil. 2 Confederencias. México: Secretaría de Educación Pública, 1942.

_____. "El maestro que se estrenó en México." El libro y el pueblo, no. 41 (Junio 1968), 31-34.

_____. "El niño y los 40 ladrones." El libro y el pueblo, no. 62 (Marzo 1970), 21-23.

_____. "El sol y la educación." El libro y el pueblo, no. 68 (Septiembre 1970), 36-37.

_____. "Literato: El niño te espera." El libro y el pueblo, no. 54 (Julio 1969), 33-35.

_____. "Posada." El libro y el pueblo, no. 70 (Noviembre 1970), 29-33.

_____. "República española en México." El libro y el pueblo, no. 29 (Junio 1967), 17-19.

_____. ¿Se comió el lobo a caperucita? Seis Conferencias para Mayores con Temas de Literatura Infantil. México: Editorial América, 1942.

_____. "Va don Quijote al colegio." El libro y el pueblo, Octubre 1968.

Ruiz Hernandez, Angelina. La literatura infantil en la escuela primaria. México: Secretaría de Educación Publica, 1963.

Salgado Corral, Ricardo. Literatura infantil en la escuela
primaria. México: Editorial Patria, 1972.

Sanchez Arrieta, María Teresa. "El club de lectura." El
libro y el pueblo, 21 (Enero-Febrero 1959), 41-49.

Secretaría de Educación Pública. El maestro. México:
Secretaría de Educación Pública, 1969.

Torner, Florentino M. La literatura en la escuela primaria.
México: E.D.I.A.P.S.A., 1940.

Torres Montalvo, Herculano Angel. "Las tendencias literarias en los adolescentes mexicanos." Revista del Instituto Nacional de Pedagogía, Octubre 1955.

Torres Quintero, Gregorio. "Los textos y la escuela de la
acción." El libro y el pueblo, 6 (Octubre, Noviembre,
Diciembre 1966), 87-88.

Trejo, Blanca Lydia. "La literatura infantil." El libro y
el pueblo, 16 (Febrero 1954), 5-22.

_____. La literatura infantil en México: Desde los Az-
tecas hasta nuestros días. México: Gráfica Moderna,
1950.

_____. "La narración del cuento infantil." El libro y
el pueblo, Septiembre-Octubre 1955.

"Un día de trabajo en una biblioteca moderna." Boletín
bibliográfico de la Escuela Nacional de Bibliotecarios
y Archivistas, Enero-Febrero 1957.

Victoria, José María. "Un bello libro al servicio de la
juventud." El libro y el pueblo, no. 54 (Julio 1969),
36-37.

Zendejas, Adelina. La crisis de la educación en México.
México: La Autora, 1958.

Books for Children and Adolescents

Abreu Gómez, Ermilo. Canek. México: Ediciones Oasis,
1972.

_____. "Ramoncito." Forjadores, Febrero 1972.

Altamirano, Ignacio M. La navidad en las montañas. México: Editorial Porrúa, 1972.

Caballero, Santos. Las aventuras de Pipiolo. México: Unión Gráfica, 1954.

Campo, Angel de. Cuentos y crónicas. México: Secretaría de Educación Pública, 1944.

Campuzano, Juan R. Jesusón. México: Secretaría de Educación Pública, 1945.

Cardona Peña, Alfredo. La máscara que hablaba. México: Secretaría de Educación Pública, 1944.

Corona, Pascuala. Cuentos mexicanos para niños. México: La Autora, 1945.

Donato, Magda. El niño de mazapán y la mariposa de cristal. México: Secretaría de Educación Pública, 1944.

Gabilondo Soler, Francisco. Album de plata. México: Editorial Cri-Crí, 1959.

_____. Album pictórico de Cri-Crí. México: El Autor, sin fecha.

_____. Las aventuras de Cri-Crí. México: El Autor, sin fecha.

_____. Los cochinitos dormilones. México: Editorial Novaro, 1967.

_____. Cuentos musicales del grillito cantor. México: El Autor, sin fecha.

_____. Cuentos y canciones de Cri-Crí. México: Selecciones del Reader's Digest, 1963.

Gastelum, Bernardo J. (ed.). Lecturas clásicas para niños. México: Secretaría de Educación Pública, 1971.

González Casanova, Pablo. Cuentos indígenas. México: Universidad Nacional Autónoma de México, 1965.

Grupo Ocelotl. Banderolas cuentos para adolescentes. México: Editorial Herrero, 1968.

_____. Cuentos para adolescentes. México: Los Autores,
1966.

_____. Entonces tuvimos miedo. México: Los Autores,
1972.

Gutiérrez Arias, Arturo, e Irene G. de Lanz. El mensaje
de Fobos. México: Los Autores, 1964.

Gutiérrez Nájera, Manuel. Cuentos, crónicas y ensayos.
México: Universidad Nacional Autónoma, 1940.

_____. Cuentos frágiles. México: Biblioteca Mínima
Mexicana, 1955.

_____. Historia de un peso falso. México: Secretaría
de Educación Pública, 1940.

_____. Los niños tristes. México: Editorial Patria,
1972.

Gutiérrez Zacarías, Flavio. Shunco. México: Topografía
Tonantzin, 1972.

Ibarra, Alfredo. Cuentos y leyendas de México. México:
Talleres Linotipográficos ACCION, 1941.

Lanz, Irene G. de. El parguito rosado. México: Editorial
A. C. A. S. I. M., 1962.

_____. Tismiche. México: Impresora Artística, S. A.,
1963.

Lizardi, José Joaquín Fernández de. El periquillo sarniento.
México: Editorial Porrúa, 1972.

Mediz Bolio, Antonio. El címbalo de oro. México: Secretaría de Educación Pública, 1971.

_____. La tierra del faisán y del venado. México:
Ediciones Botas, 1944.

Mendoza, Vicente T. Lírica infantil de México. México:
El Colegio de México, 1951.

Nájera, Indiana. El átomo que tenía catarro. México: La
Autora, 1962.

_____. Carne viva. México: La Autora, 1943.

_____. La gota de agua que se aburría. México: La
Autora, 1963.

_____. La hormiguita revoltosa. México: La Autora,
1963.

Nervo, Amado. El dominio del Canadá. México: Editorial
Patria, 1972.

_____. Lecturas literarias. México: Editorial Patria,
1972.

_____. Obras completas. Madrid: Biblioteca Nueva,
1927.

Peza, Juan de Dios. Cantos del hogar. México: Editores
Mexicanos Unidos, 1966.

Robles, Antonio. Cuentos para la escuela primaria. México: Ediciones Oasis, 1968.

_____. Historias de Azulita y Rompetacones. México:
Secretaría de Educación Pública, 1968.

_____. Ocho estrellas y ocho cenzontles. México: Edi-
ciones Oasis, 1954.

_____. Rompetacones y 100 cuentos más. México:
Secretaría de Educación Pública, 1962.

_____. Rompetacones y 100 cuentos más. México: Edi-
ciones Oasis, 1968.

_____. Un gorrión en las guerras de las fieras. Méxi-
co: Secretaría de Educación Pública, 1942.

Rosas, José. Lecciones de moral en verso. México:
Murgia, 1877.

_____. Libro de la infancia. México: Antigua Imprenta
de Murguia, 1893.

Rosas Moreno, José. 50 fábulas de José Rosas Moreno.
México: Editorial Surco, 1943.

Serradell, Luz María. Adivina ... Adivina.... México:
La Autora, 1961.

_____. Alas inquietas. México: La Autora, 1970.

_____. Manojito de flores. México: La Autora, 1964.

_____. Te voy a contar un cuento. México: La Autora,
1970.

Serrano Martinez, Celedonio. El cazador y sus perros.
México: Luis Fernandez, 1959.

Stefano, Blanca de. Noriki. México: Editorial Patria,
1953.

Tablada, José Juan. La nieve viajera. México: Editorial
Patria, 1972.

Trejo, Blanca Lydia. Copo de algodón. México: La Autora, 1955.

_____. El quetzal. México: La Autora, 1955.

_____. El ratón Panchito roe libros. México: La Au-
tora, 1957.

_____. La marimba. México: La Autora, 1957.

_____. La pícara sabelotodo. México: La Autora, 1956.

_____. Leyendas mexicanas para los niños. México:
La Autora, 1959.

_____. Lo que sucedió al nopal. México: La Autora,
1956.

_____. Maravillas de un colmenar. México: La Autora,
1954.

Von Glumer, Berta. El niño ante la nautraleza. Puebla:
Editorial Emilio Wirth, 1965.

_____. Rimas y juegos digitales. México: Imprenta
Unión, 1964.

Zendejas, Josefina. El caminito dorado. México: Guerrero Hermanos, 1931.

_____. Cuentos. México: Oaxaca 80, 1936.

_____. El múneco de nieve. México: La Autora, sin fecha.

_____. Vidas mínimas. México: La Autora, 1941.

Other Sources

América en cifras 1972, situación cultural: Educación y otros aspectos. Washington, D.C.: Organización de los Estados Americanos, 1973.

América en cifras 1974, situación cultural: Educación y otros aspectos. Washington, D.C.: Organización de los Estados Americanos, 1974.

América en cifras 1974, situación económica: 5 precios, salarios, consumo, y otros aspectos económicos. Washington, D.C.: Organización de los Estados Americanos, 1974.

Lanz, Irene G. de. Conversation with the author on May 18, 1973, in Mexico City at a private hospital.

Palacios, Miguel. Conversation with the author on May 14, 1973, at the Biblioteca México, Mexico City.

Wilkie, James W., ed. Statistical abstract of Latin America. Vol. 17 (1976). Los Angeles: University of California, 1976.

APPENDIX C

A HEARTFELT PLEA: NOTES ON BOOKS
FOR CHILDREN AND ADOLESCENTS FROM SPAIN*

Through many years of accepted misconceptions librarians and teachers have traditionally ignored Spanish literature for children and adolescents. This has resulted in a great cultural loss for many Chicano, Mexican-American, and/or Spanish-speaking young people. After careful consideration of the objectives by Chicano educators and bilingual librarians, I cannot help but implore all concerned with the literature for children and adolescents to seriously examine the wealth of literature from Spain for young people.

Some of the commonly accepted fallacies by teachers and librarians are that Mexican-American and/or Spanish-speaking children and adolescents cannot understand the Spanish language that is spoken in Spain, that Chicano young people cannot "relate" to the difference in backgrounds and traditions, and that there is very little literature for children and adolescents written in Spanish. I believe that they are wrong. And because more and more young people are gaining a new pride and awareness in their history and background, there is a growing demand for books written in Spanish, but public libraries and school libraries have embarrassingly small col-

*Reprinted by permission from English Journal 66:49-52 (March 1977). Copyright © 1977 by the National Council of Teachers of English.

lections of books written in Spanish.

To insist on guidelines for children's literature is
aesthetically and intellectually dishonest, but to ignore the
literary and artistic qualities of books from Spain is an un-
just treatment of one culture. I propose that we evaluate
books for their literary quality rather than for the "messages"
of their content and the ethnic qualities of their characters.
Yet, many times poor translations of American books for
children, or inferior selections, have encouraged mediocrity
in the literature available for children and adolescents in
Spanish. I believe that we should select books that are considered good literature and that are worthwhile and appropriate
for all children and adolescents.

Several studies have reminded us of the questionable
validity of subjective adult judgments concerning the reading
preferences of children.[1] Yet, why not offer an honest,
serious, real selection of literature for children and adolescents written in Spanish? I believe that when books from
Spain are carefully selected, Chicano, Mexican-American
and/or Spanish-speaking children and adolescents may en-
hance the essential dignity and integrity of their backgrounds
and may acquire appreciation and understanding of their own
culture.

Several authors have criticized children's books from
Spain. They reprove the lack of imaginative variety in
stories and illustrations, the small percentage of good non-
fiction books, and the relative expensiveness of better editions.[2] Even though I agree with some of their criticisms,
I cannot help but insist that the books available in Spain are
unknown treasures for those children and adolescents who
want to read in Spanish. The following is a brief sample of
Spanish books that could also be enjoyed by children and adolescents in the U.S.

Picture Books

Excellent illustrations and simple texts make Spanish picture books a delight for the pre-schoolers. La familia, by Antonio Jiménez-Landi Martínez (Aguilar, 1974), describes the extended Spanish family and the feelings of refinement that are encouraged in Spanish children. Rita en la cocina de su abuela, by Rita Culla (Juventud, 1971), shows Rita comparing her grandmother's simple, town kitchen with her mother's new plastic kitchen with its modern appliances. Circus activities including a parade, magicians, tigers, elephants and acrobats are pleasingly portrayed in El circo, by Antonio Jiménez-Landi Martínez (Aguilar, 1972). Amelia Benet describes the life of typical Spanish children in their daily-life activities and the change of seasons in Miguel en invierno (Juventud, 1970), Mireya en otoño (Juventud, 1969), Silvia y Miguel en verano (Juventud, 1970), and David y los tulipanes (Juventud, 1969). Chitina y su gato, by Montserrat del Amo (Juventud, 1970), is a delightfully illustrated story of Chitina and her adventures with her cat. Modern illustrations of zoo animals that have been given back their freedom are shown in Si yo hiciese un parque, by Eulalia Valeri (La Galera, 1965). Spanish children are described as they use a public library in Entre juego y juego ... ¡un libro! by Aurora Díaz-Plaja (La Galera, 1967). Todos tenemos hermanos pequeños, by José María Espinas (La Galera, 1968), understandingly sympathizes with abnormal children. Fantasy and humor are combined in Antonio Cuadrench's Los tres caballeros altos (La Galera, 1972) to solve the problem of a king and his lazy kingdom.

Fiction: Kindergarten through Second Grades

There is a wide selection of attractive animal stories with charming illustrations.   Some of the outstanding animal stories that children may enjoy are Mañana de parque, by Jaime Ferrán (Anaya, 1972); Tula la tortuga, by María Angeles Olle (La Galera, 1964); Mi gorrión, by María Angeles Olle (La Galera, 1964); and Silencio en el bosque, by Montserrat Mussons (La Galera, 1969).

Children at play are shown in delightful settings and imaginative situations.   For various playful occasions children may read Cien nuevos cuentos, by Juan Antonio de la Iglesia (Ediciones Recreativas, 1969); El pájaro pinto y otras cosas, by Carola Soler Arce (Aguilar, 1954); El globo de papel, by Elisa Vives de Fábregas (La Galera, 1973); El tren que perdió una rueda, by Concepción Roca (La Galera, 1972); and El caballito que quería volar, by Marta Osorio (La Galera, 1968).

Gorgeous illustrations and simple texts present colors in their natural conditions in María Luisa Jover's Yo soy el amarillo (La Galera, 1968), Yo soy el rojo (La Galera, 1968), and Yo soy el azul (La Galera, 1969).

The daily adventures of a Spanish family and their lives with a traveling circus are originally portrayed in black-and-white cartoons by María Luisa Gefaell in Antón Retaco, la función (Narcea, 1972), Antón Retaco, por los caminos (Narcea, 1962), Antón Retaco, en villavieja (Narcea, 1973), Antón Retaco, los niños tristes (Narcea, 1973), and Antón Retaco, del ancho mundo (Narcea, 1973).

Fiction: Third through Sixth Grades

There are many graceful stories that describe the

feelings, thoughts, adventures and interests of Spanish children that can captivate all children. Ana, by María Luisa
Sola (La Galera, 1973), shows a typical girl in slacks, long
hair, tennis racket, guitar, records and all the joys and
problems of spending her summer holidays with her aunt,
uncle and cousins. Un castillo en el camino, by María Mar-
cela Sanchez Coquillat (Juventud, 1972), is an original story
of two Spanish well-to-do families and their daily activities.
Celia en el colegio, by Elena Fortun (Aguilar, 1973), shows
Celia's mischiefs at a parochial school. Roque el trapero,
by José Vallverdú Aixala (La Galera, 1971), describes the
life of a poor Spanish boy, the difficulties of his work, and
his hopes for the future.

The following are several outstanding adventure stories
that can enthrall young readers with their intriguing dialogues
and engrossing excitement: Aparecen los blok, by Montserrat del Amo (Juventud, 1971); Han raptado a ney, by Mar-
cela Sanchez Coquillat (Juventud, 1972); Los blok y la bici-
cleta fantasma, by Montserrat del Amo (Juventud, 1973); La
pandilla de los diez, by Joaquín Carbo (La Galera, 1969);
Cuentos de siempre, by Mariano Hispano (Afha Internacional,
1974); Aventura en Australia, by Mariano Hispano (Plaza
and Janés, 1973); and by Carmen Kuntz, Oscar y los
hombres rana (Lumen, 1973), Oscar, espía atómico (Juventud, 1970), Oscar espeleólogo (Lumen, 1973), and Oscar en
Africa (Juventud, 1974).

Animal stories that may appeal to older children by
their descriptions of animals in their natural settings are
Ladis, un gran pequeño, by José María Sanchez-Silva (Mar-
fil, 1971); El zoo de pitus, by Sebastián Sorribas (La Galera,
1974); La fuerza de la gacela, by Carmen Vazquez Vigo (Doncel, 1964); Rikki-Tikki, by Manuel Maristany (Doncel, 1969);

and Caramelos de menta, by Carmen Vazquez Vigo (Doncel, 1973).

Fiction: Seventh through Ninth Grades

There does not appear to be a large selection of novels for adolescents in Spain. Violence, sex and drugs are never mentioned. But there are a few that may interest young adults: El gato de los ojos de color de oro, by Marta Osorio (Doncel, 1965), describes the daily life of a Spanish Gypsy family, their concerns and joys. Landa, el valín, by Carlos María Ydígoras (Doncel, 1969), narrates, through the eyes of a 12-year-old orphan, the social conditions of miners in Spain. It emphasizes the miners' lack of safety, their poverty, and their deep family loyalty. Polvorón, by José Vallverdú Aixala (La Galera, 1973), is an interesting story about a dog and its many adventures on a Spanish farm. Dardo, el caballo del bosque, by Rafael Morales (Doncel, 1970), describes the strong affection between a boy and his horse, Dardo.

Science Fiction

Science fiction is also popular among young Spanish readers. Los astronautas del "Mochuelo," by Sebastián Sorribas y Roig (La Galera, 1972), has exciting adventures in space with a crew of teenagers. Oscar y corazón de púrpura, by Carmen Kurtz, is a fast-moving science-fiction story of gangsters and deep teenage friendships.

Biographies

Splendid biographies of great authors and artists have been written for adolescents in Spanish: Cervantes, by Isabel

Flores de Lemus, is an outstanding biography of Cervantes.
It is a marvelous introduction to Cervantes, his time, and
his works. La extraordinaria vida de Picasso, by José Palau
y Fabré (Aymá, 1972), explains, primarily, Picasso's artistic development. El terrible florentino, by María Pilar
Llorente (Doncel, 1973), is an excellent biography with gorgeous illustrations of Michelangelo's finest works. Vida del
Joven Andersen, by Mariano Tudela (Doncel, 1963), describes
the early years of the Danish author.

Classics

Spanish literary masterpieces have been charmingly
adapted for adolescents. Aventuras de don Quijote de la
mancha, by Miguel de Cervantes Saavedra (Edaf, 1972), has
maintained the enchanting dialogue in this superb adaptation
with beautiful illustrations of Don Quijote's adventures.
Poema del Cid, adapted by María Luisa Gefaell (Noquer,
1970), pleasingly illustrates the life and philosophy of the
famous 12th-century Spanish knight. El lazarillo de tormes,
by Diego Hurtado de Mendoza (Afha Internacional, 1975), is
a marvelous adaptation with delightful illustrations of this
famous picaresque Spanish novel of the 16th century.

Historical Fiction

The history of Spain has been exquisitely portrayed
for adolescents in historical novels of Spain of the Feudal and
Middle Ages. El juglar del Cid, adapted by Joaquín Aguirre
Bellver (Doncel, 1960), is a fascinating description of the
famous Spanish errant knight, Ruy Díaz. Balada de un cas-
tellano, by María Isabel Molina (Doncel, 1970), shows the
intrigues, life, and customs of the Moors and Christians in

the year 990. Un muchacho sefaradí, by Carmen Pérez Avel-
lo (Doncel, 1968), is an unusual narrative of the exile of the
Jews from Spain in 1492.

Poetry, Theater, and Songs

There are many imaginative, graceful poetry books
that can be enjoyed by all children. The following editions
include pleasing poems with beautiful illustrations: El hada
acaramelada, by Gloria Fuertes (Igreca de Ediciones, 1973);
El silbo del aire, two volumes edited by Arturo Medina (Vi-
cens-Vives, 1971); Alegrías-poemas para niños, by Marina
Romero (Anaya, 1972); and El sol, la luna y las estrellas,
by Salvador de Madariaga (Juventud, 1960).

Títeres con cachiporra, by Angeles Gasset (Aguilar,
1969), includes five pleasing puppet dramatizations that may
be performed at school. Canciones de España y América,
selected by Francisco Ribes (Santillana, 1965), includes
splendid illustrations and fifty-six popular Spanish and Latin
American songs for children.

Fables and Legends

The marvelous folklore of Spain can be appreciated
through its fables and legends. Fábulas, by Felix María
Samaniego (Veron, 1972), is a delightful collection of short
fables with lovely illustrations. Leyendas de España, by
Antonio Jiménez-Landi Martínez (Aguilar, 1971), is a splendid collection of Spanish legends of the Middle Ages and the
Renaissance Period with handsome illustrations.

Religious Stories

There is a vast amount of saccharine, moralistic,

religious literature for children and adolescents in Spain.
Innumerable stories that emphasize the religious way of life
and the importance of God in children's lives have been ap-
proved by the powerful Spanish ecclesiastical censure.

Even though the literature for children and adolescents
from Spain may be criticized from many points of view, I
believe that it offers the pleasure, enjoyment and variety
that is very much needed by young readers who want or need
to read in Spanish. My heartfelt plea to librarians and
teachers is that they should offer a diversified selection of
literature in Spanish to Spanish-speaking children and adolescents, so that young readers may acquire a genuine pride in
their cultural heritage and an enjoyable introduction to literature written expressly for children and adolescents in Spanish.

Notes

[1]Okada, Masahito and Howard J. Sullivan. Type of
Story-Setting Preferred by Inner-City Children. Paper presented at the American Educational Research Association annual meeting, February 1971.

[2]Pellowski, Anne. The World of Children's Literature. (New York: R. R. Bowker, 1968), p. 77.

AUTHOR INDEX

149

TITLE INDEX